OF LEARNED IGNORANCE

of
learned
ignorance

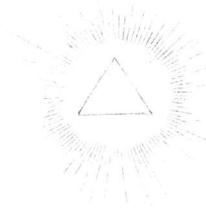

BY NICOLAS CUSANUS

Translated by Germain Heron
Introduction by D. J. B. Hawkins

Angelico Press

This Angelico Press edition is a reprint
of the work originally published in
1954 by Yale University Press.

For information, address:
Angelico Press, Ltd.
169 Monitor St.
Brooklyn, NY 11222
www.angelicopress.com

Ppr: 979-8-88677-046-9
Cloth: 979-8-88677-047-6

Cover design
by Michael Schrauzer

CONTENTS

INTRODUCTION   *page* ix

DEDICATION   3

THE FIRST BOOK

    I. HOW KNOWLEDGE IS IGNORANCE   7

  II. PRELIMINARY EXPLANATION OF ALL THAT
FOLLOWS   9

 III. ABSOLUTE TRUTH IS BEYOND OUR GRASP   11

 IV. THE ABSOLUTE MAXIMUM IS KNOWN BUT NOT
UNDERSTOOD MAXIMUM AND MINIMUM ARE
SYNONYMOUS   12

  V. ONENESS OF THE MAXIMUM   14

 VI. THE MAXIMUM IS ABSOLUTE NECESSITY   16

 VII. ETERNAL UNITY AND TRINITY   17

VIII. ETERNAL GENERATION   20

 IX. ETERNAL PROCESSION OF THE CONNECTION   21

  X. HOW THE UNDERSTANDING OF THE TRINITY
IN UNITY TRANSCENDS ALL THINGS   22

 XI. MATHEMATICS ARE A VERY GREAT HELP IN
THE UNDERSTANDING OF DIFFERENT DIVINE
TRUTHS   25

XII. THE WAY IN WHICH MATHEMATICAL SIGNS
SHOULD BE USED FOR OUR PURPOSE   27

CONTENTS

XIII. MODIFICATIONS OF THE ABSOLUTE INFINITE
LINE   *page* 28

XIV. THE INFINITE LINE IS A TRIANGLE   30

XV. THE INFINITE TRIANGLE IS A CIRCLE AND A
SPHERE   32

XVI. THE RELATIONSHIP OF THE MAXIMUM TO ALL
THINGS IS BY ANALOGY WHAT THE INFINITE
IS TO LINES   34

XVII. PROFOUND TRUTHS FROM THE PRECEDING
CONSIDERATION   36

XVIII. FROM THE SAME CONSIDERATION WE LEARN
THE MEANING OF THE PARTICIPATION OF
BEING   39

XIX. ANALOGY BETWEEN THE INFINITE TRIANGLE
AND THE INFINITE TRINITY   41

XX. TEACHING ON THE TRINITY CONTINUED: IM-
POSSIBILITY OF HAVING FOUR OR MORE
DIVINE PERSONS   44

XXI. ANALOGY BETWEEN THE INFINITE CIRCLE AND
UNITY   46

XXII. IN THE PROVIDENCE OF GOD CONTRADIC-
TORIES ARE RECONCILED   49

XXIII. ANALOGY OF THE INFINITE SPHERE AND THE
ACTUAL EXISTENCE OF GOD   51

XXIV. NAME OF GOD AND POSITIVE THEOLOGY   53

XXV. VARIOUS ANTHROPOMORPHISMS USED BY
PAGANS   57

XXVI. NEGATIVE THEOLOGY   59

CONTENTS

THE SECOND BOOK

PROLOGUE *page* 65

I. FROM PROPOSITIONS ALREADY ESTABLISHED THE UNITY AND INFINITY OF THE UNIVERSE IS INFERRED 67

II. THE BEING OF A CREATURE COMES IN A MYSTERIOUS WAY FROM THE BEING OF THE MAXIMUM 71

III. IN A MYSTERIOUS WAY THE MAXIMUM ENVELOPES AND DEVELOPS ALL THINGS 75

IV. HOW THE UNIVERSE, WHICH IS ONLY A RESTRICTED FORM OF MAXIMUM, IS A LIKENESS OF THE ABSOLUTE 80

V. EVERYTHING IN EVERYTHING 83

VI. THE UNIVERSE—ITS UNITY AND DEGREES OF DEVELOPMENT 86

VII. THE TRINITY OF THE UNIVERSE 89

VIII. POSSIBILITY OR MATTER OF THE UNIVERSE 92

IX. THE SOUL OR FORM OF THE UNIVERSE 97

X. SPIRIT OF THE UNIVERSE 103

XI. COROLLARIES ON MOVEMENT 107

XII. CONDITIONS OF THE EARTH 111

XIII. DIVINE DESIGN IN THE CREATION OF THE WORLD AND ITS CONSTITUENT PARTS IS WHOLLY ADMIRABLE 118

THE THIRD BOOK

PROLOGUE 125

I. THE UNSURPASSABLE MAXIMUM, EVEN IF LIMITED TO THIS OR THAT GENUS OR SPECIES, CAN EXIST ONLY IN THE ABSOLUTE 127

CONTENTS

II. THE MAXIMUM AS LIMITED AND ABSOLUTE TOGETHER, AT ONCE CREATOR AND CREATURE *page* 131

III. HUMAN NATURE AND ONLY HUMAN NATURE PECULIARLY ADAPTED TO BE THIS MAXIMUM 134

IV. THIS BEING IS JESUS, EVER BLESSED, GOD AND MAN 138

V. THAT CHRIST WAS CONCEIVED OF THE HOLY GHOST AND WAS BORN OF THE VIRGIN MARY 141

VI. THE MYSTERY OF JESUS' DEATH 144

VII. THE MYSTERY OF THE RESURRECTION 147

VIII. CHRIST THE FIRST-FRUITS FROM THE DEAD, ASCENDED INTO HEAVEN 151

IX. CHRIST, THE JUDGE OF THE LIVING AND THE DEAD 154

X. THE JUDGE'S SENTENCE 157

XI. THE MYSTERIES OF FAITH 160

XII. THE CHURCH 166

LETTER OF THE AUTHOR TO THE LORD CARDINAL JULIAN 173

INTRODUCTION

THE MORE COMPREHENSIVE A PHILOSOPHY tries to be, the sooner it finds itself at the border-land of mystery. Some philosophers there are, and many in our own time, who actively resent the mysterious and seek to enclose themselves in a self-contained human edifice with no windows on a wider world. Such an edifice must be built of words understood in a way in which the word is not, as for Heidegger, the dwelling-place of being but an arbitrary counter in a purely human game. Their philosophy becomes a higher lexicography, a dictionary-making which is by no means without its own interest but is hardly an adequate representative of the functions which men have hitherto assigned to philosophy. They are the contemporary counterparts of the minute philosophers whom Berkeley rebukes in *Alciphron*.

More reasonably the philosophers of the main stream have usually tried to map as much of the realm of being as they could and to draw the frontiers beyond which they were unable to penetrate. But there are others who, like Sir Thomas Browne, find philosophical truth always double-faced and love to be paradoxical, to lose themselves in a mystery, and to pursue their reason to an O *altitudo!* In our own day it is at the entrance to philosophy itself that, according to Gabriel Marcel, problems end and mysteries begin, and existentialists

in general have done much—too much, some of us would say
—to disturb our satisfaction with the progress of knowledge
and to restore the sense of the mystery of being.

The great fifteenth-century representative of the philosophy
of paradox is Nicholas of Cusa. Although he is in some ways
profoundly original, it is also true to say that there re-emerges
in him a current of thought, derived from the more esoteric
elements of Neoplatonism, which pursued its course through
the middle ages in a mainly underground fashion, manifesting
itself only at intervals in thinkers such as John Scotus Erigena
and Master Eckhart. The ruling philosophical tradition of the
middle ages had been a persistent intellectualism, typified by
the thought of St. Thomas Aquinas, in which every effort was
made to convert mysteries into problems and to solve the problems themselves by the methods of rational analysis and inference. St. Thomas was ready enough to acknowledge a mystery
when such efforts proved unavailing, but the resources of
reason had to be fully exploited first.

The completeness with which Thomistic intellectualism had
ceased to be a living issue in the fifteenth century is one thing
which surprises us when we consider the fortunes of Nicholas
of Cusa. Barely two centuries had elapsed since Thomism, and
other systems similar in spirit, had victoriously established
themselves, and the universities continued to be dominated by
Thomists, Scotists, and Terminists. But the work of the
Terminists, however justified some of their questions and
criticisms may have been, does seem very rapidly to have shaken
men's confidence in the possibility of a valid metaphysical
synthesis of the Thomist kind. Scholastic theology, together
with the philosophy involved in it, had become enmeshed in
the arid verbal controversies which led Thomas à Kempis to
rebuke the theologians who engaged in high-flown disputes
about the Trinity without caring whether they were themselves
pleasing to the Trinity or not. Thus, for all its piety and acute-

ness, the *Imitation of Christ* prepared the way for a new spirituality, divorced from theology, which, being neither contemplative nor active, tended perforce to be merely emotional. Thomism was eminently capable of revival, and it revived not only in modern times but already in the sixteenth and seventeenth centuries during the period from Cajetan to John of St. Thomas, but the scholasticism of the fifteenth century seems to have been little more than a verbal game.

Otherwise it would be difficult to explain how small was the opposition provoked by the quite different kind of system proposed by Nicholas of Cusa. It is true that, in answer to the *De Docta Ignorantia*, Johannes Wenck of the university of Heidelberg produced his *De Ignota Litteratura*, but in the *Apologia Doctae Ignorantiae* Nicholas brushed him aside in a very confident and almost high-handed way, and sailed on the course of his ecclesiastical career without further contradiction. The spirit of the Renaissance was already abroad in Italy and in Rome, and there was as yet none of the fear of novelty to be aroused by the Reformation. Men were ready for something new and striking. Not that Nicholas ever had any great following, but he was a highly respectable and respected figure as Cardinal and Bishop of Brixen, while his philosophy, for all its connection with Erigena and Eckhart, belonged to the dawning Renaissance. It is quite in character that, on his delightful monument by Andrea Bregno in his titular church of San Pietro in Vincoli at Rome, Nicholas does homage to a thoroughly neo-classic St. Peter in the presence of a typically early Renaissance angel.

II

Nicholas's speculations were the by-product of a busy life of ecclesiastical diplomacy and administration. He was born in 1401 at Cues, opposite Berncastel on the Moselle, and we might like to think that his literary inspiration was fortified by good Berncastler. But the stories of his father's unkindness suggest that he may have been sparingly supplied with it. This father, Johann Cryfts or Krypffs, belonged to the rising commercial classes; he was a prosperous boatowner who also accumulated a substantial amount of property on land. He apparently had no use for his studious son, who fled from his severities to the protection of Count Theodoric von Manderscheid, who is said to have sent Nicholas to the celebrated school at Deventer conducted by the Brothers of the Common Life. It is certain, at any rate, that Nicholas entered the university of Heidelberg in 1416 and went on to Padua in 1417, where he took his doctorate in canon law in 1423. On returning to the Rhineland he was beneficed by the Archbishop of Treves, and he would presumably have passed his life in dealing with ecclesiastical affairs on his native soil if he had not been taken as secretary by Cardinal Giordano Orsini, then legate in Germany, and been brought into contact with the Council of Basle.

Cardinal Cesarini, who presided as papal legate over the Council of Basle, now became Nicholas's friend and patron. The problems before the Council included not only those of church reform in general but, in particular, how to avoid any repetition of the Great Schism which had so recently been healed. Many at Basle thought that the solution lay in an ultimate supremacy of a general council over the papacy, and Nicholas was originally of this opinion, but experience of the interminable dissensions and practical ineffectiveness of the discussions at Basle seems to have convinced him that the papacy was the only institution strong enough to ensure peace and order in the Church. Hence, in 1437, he entered the direct service of Pope Eugenius IV. Thereafter he was employed in missions in Germany and in the negotiations with the Eastern Church which culminated in the short-lived reunion of East and West proclaimed at the Council of Florence in 1438.

Nicholas of Cusa was made a Cardinal by the humanist Pope Nicholas V in 1448 and Bishop of Brixen in 1450. His business in the Tyrol, apart from general reforms, was to assert the independence of the Tyrolese bishoprics against the dominance of Sigismund of Hapsburg. In this he met with only partial success, and from 1458 onwards he was once more at the side of the new Pope, Pius II, who was his old friend Aeneas Sylvius Piccolomini. While busying himself with the always troubled affairs of the church in Bohemia and on his way to confer with the Pope at Ancona, he was taken ill at Todi and died there on 11th August 1464.

In his practical activity Nicholas was obviously a sincere and earnest reformer, and, if there had been more churchmen like him in the fifteenth century, the tragedy of the disruption of Europe in the sixteenth century might have been avoided. Most of his works are brief and, apart from those which deal with contemporary ecclesiastical problems or with matters of scientific interest, are mainly concerned to recapitulate and to commend the ideas which emerged once and for all in the treatise *De Docta Ignorantia* completed in 1440. Such are, for example, *De Coniecturis*, *De Possest* and *De Venatione Sapientiae*. The reader who comes fresh to Nicholas of Cusa may be heartened by the fact that the whole of Nicholas's system is contained in the *De Docta Ignorantia*, but he will require some assistance with a thought which is often elusive and a terminology which is often obscure.

III

In the concluding words of the book Nicholas tells his patron, Cardinal Cesarini, that his system came to him with a sudden illumination when he was making a return voyage from Greece. This was the occasion when he formed part of a papal mission to escort Emperor John VI Palaeologus, the Patriarch of Constantinople and a large delegation of Eastern bishops and theologians to Europe in order to negotiate that reunion of the Eastern and Western churches which was eventually brought about at the Council of Florence. During the long voyage from Constantinople to Venice, which lasted from November 1437 to February 1438, he must indeed have had plenty of time for meditation. But what exactly was the discovery that he made at this period? The general plan of the book is not very original; it follows the customary Neoplatonic scheme of the outflow of things from God and their return to him which had been represented in the earlier middle ages, for example, by the *De Divisione Naturae* of John Scotus Erigena. The notion of the reconciliation of contraries in God, the *coincidentia oppositorum*, is fairly evidently derived from Eckhart. The theory of enlightened ignorance, the *docta ignorantia* itself, is only a new expression and extension of the *theologia negativa* which was familiar enough to all mediaeval thinkers, especially as found in the writings of the Pseudo-Dionysius.

Nicholas does not tell us what precisely he regarded as his special inspiration, but we might well suppose that it was the way in which these elements fitted together, for it is in this respect that he is really original. Every thinker knows the kind of flash in which factors hitherto disparate suddenly take shape and present themselves as a whole, and, even if the particular factors by themselves are derivative, it is not too much to describe their synthesis as a moment of illumination. We may reconstruct Nicholas's philosophical history in not too improbable a way. In mediaeval universities he would have been brought up in the tradition of Aristotelian scholasticism. This current of thought had had its hour of triumph in the thirteenth century with St. Thomas and his contemporaries, but its positive achievements had been subjected to a process of whittling away by the criticism of the Terminists from William of Ockham onwards. The metaphysics presented to Nicholas in the fifteenth century might well have impressed themselves on his mind as a collection of sterile logomachies incapable of satisfying him either as a philosopher or as a sincerely religious man. Meanwhile he retained the memory of his early studies at Deventer, when he had been introduced to authors such as the Pseudo-Dionysius, Erigena and Eckhart. Perhaps they were really more to the point than the niggling logicians. But the logicians, after all, were logicians and had the advantage of an exact and acknowledged logical method. The problem was to devise a logical approach which would lead to and justify the intuitions of the mediaeval Platonists. The version of the *theologia negativa* presented by Nicholas in his book must have come to his mind as the solution of the difficulty. He could now at last offer systematically and with confidence what he had hitherto suspected to be true but had been unable to substantiate in a form capable of withstanding criticism.

Nicholas sets out the plan of the *De Docta Ignorantia* in the second chapter of the first book. All three books are going to deal with a *maximum* but in different senses. The first book is concerned with the *maximum absolutum*, which is God, the second with the *maximum contractum*, the sum of limited things which is the universe, and the third with the *maximum* within the universe, that created nature in which the universe as a whole is fulfilled and which links the world with its creator. This is the human nature of the Incarnate Word; in Christ there is personal and existential identity of the *maximum absolutum* and the *maximum contractum*. The third book belongs, therefore, to Christian theology, and we are faced with another preliminary question about the character of the whole work. Did Nicholas suppose that in what he had to say about the Incarnation, as well as in his speculations about the Trinity in the first book, he was endowing these doctrines with rational necessity and thus incorporating them into the sphere of philosophy? If not, how does he draw the line between philosophical and revealed theology?

The short answer is that these questions are anachronistic in form and have, as thus expressed, very little bearing upon the main stream of mediaeval thought. It was in later times that the Christian thinker's need to define his position against various classes of opponents made him lay more and more stress on the distinction between those of his beliefs which could be defended on general grounds of philosophical reason and those for which the appeal could only be to an historical revelation. The distinction was not alien to the mediaeval mind, and St. Thomas, for instance, was careful to make it on particular occasions, but the emphasis was not the same. The impulse of mediaeval thought was still the faith seeking understanding (*fides quaerens intellectum*) of St. Anselm. The Christian faith had established itself by means of signs declaring its divine origin and, along with the facts of common sense and the accepted conclusions of the sciences, entered into the sum total of facts to be philosophized about. The intellectual ideal was an ever deeper understanding and more closely knit rational synthesis of all these facts. Even when St. Thomas is defending Christianity in the *Summa contra Gentiles*, he is hardly at all concerned with showing its historical credentials; his aim is to exhibit as clearly as possible the rationality of the beliefs held by Christians. For the *Contra Gentiles* is neither more nor less a *summa philosophica* than the *Summa Theologica*; both are organic syntheses of what we might now distinguish as philosophy and theology.

So, with Nicholas of Cusa, there is no reason to doubt that he would have agreed that the Trinity and the Incarnation were and remained doctrines of an historical revelation, with some reserves in favour of a Pythagorean acknowledgment of the Trinity, and that they were, therefore, on a different plane from his purely philosophical matter, but he would not have supposed this distinction to have much to do with his purpose. His purpose was to sketch a metaphysical synthesis which would embrace the deliverances both of reason and of faith. It is as such that his work must be judged in the context of its time.

IV

In the first book of the *De Docta Ignorantia*, which deals with God in himself, the principle of enlightened ignorance makes its appearance at once and receives its principal application. From some early remarks on reasoning it might appear that Nicholas was going to depreciate the value of inference and to grade conclusions in accordance with their distance from first premises in a decreasing order of certainty (I, 1). But this is not the real point. Nicholas is not moved by a consideration of propositions, which are simply either true or false, but by the truth of notions or their adequacy to the subjects to which they are attributed. Here we can speak of degrees of truth according to the extent to which they reveal the nature of the subject. And here, says Nicholas, we must always speak of degrees of truth wherever the subject is not directly known. For we can know things indirectly only if they are similar to things which we know directly, and things, he holds, are never exactly similar. That is why philosophers have been so patently unsuccessful in their search for the exact quiddity or nature of things (I, 3). In other words, the knowledge of anything by description must be based on the knowledge of something else by acquaintance, but, since no two things are exactly similar, the description which we apply to the thing indirectly known can only apply to it approximately and inadequately. Hence our partial knowledge of it implies at the same time a confession of partial ignorance, and without such enlightened ignorance we should be guilty of genuine error in claiming to know of it more than we really know. All our inferential knowledge, then, is by comparisons and similarities, and it is never more than proportionately true in the sense explained, that is, in proportion to the degree of similarity which the inferred object bears to objects of acquaintance.

When we apply this principle to God, considered as the absolute maximum, it is evident that God infinitely exceeds any object of natural experience and is, therefore, infinitely incomprehensible. Such a statement no more implies complete agnosticism than similar statements by less paradoxical writers. It is clear that, according to Nicholas, we do know that God exists and that he is the absolute maximum, and there is more to be said about God in the sequel, but beyond all this there is an unlimited field for the confession of enlightened ignorance.

We are impelled to ask how Nicholas supposes us to know that God exists. In reality this does not appear to be a central question for him, and he deals with it only in a kind of digression from his main argument about the nature of God (I, 6). For Nicholas thinks of existence as a predicate derived from the things of experience and, consequently, applicable only in an inadequate way to God. He expressly says that we may think of God as existent or as non-existent or as both existent and non-existent or as neither existent nor non-existent. In each case, however, we are presupposing the maximum of truth as the subject which we are clumsily trying to characterize, and that maximum of truth is God. Thus we cannot but affirm God, whatever we may say about him and however inadequate this may be. This is plainly in the general line of the ontological argument. Nicholas has already defined God in the Anselmian manner as that than which there can be nothing greater and holds that to think of such a maximum is necessarily to affirm it, however much enlightened ignorance may affect the validity of the predicates which we attribute to it. He does, however, also indicate the causal argument in a single sentence, saying that everything else must be derived from the maximum and, therefore, nothing else could be if the maximum were not. But his implicit acceptance of existence as a predicate explains why he prefers to speak of God not in terms of *ens* or *esse* or even as *maximum ens* but simply as the *maximum*.

Nicholas's way of progress in the knowledge of God without overlooking the divine incomprehensibility is by perceiving in God the reconciliation of contraries (*coincidentia oppositorum*). He illustrates his contention chiefly by means of mathematical examples (I, 11–21). Like many other thinkers he was genuinely persuaded that there was in the end something mystical about mathematics, and at the outset of his work he commends Pythagoras for having acknowledged the universal significance of number and proportion (I, 1). So he tells us that, when corporeal quantity is left aside, the maximum must coincide with the minimum, for the maximum is the extreme of greatness and the minimum is the extreme of littleness, and greatness and littleness belong to the category of quantity applicable to corporeal things. He maintains with great ingenuity of argument that an infinite line coincides with an infinite triangle, an infinite circle and an infinite sphere. Which things are an allegory, for they are symbols taken from the clearest kind of knowledge that we possess in order to exemplify how opposites are reconciled in the absolute unity of God.

There are not many who are likely to take all this very seriously as an adumbration of ultimate mystery. Some will be irresistably reminded of Lewis Carroll, and others may despise what seems to be no more than conjuring with words. The best way of putting in a word for Nicholas is perhaps to suggest temperately that he is not altogether talking nonsense. That he is attempting to use essentially finite concepts outside their finite frame of reference is true enough, and Kant could readily point out that class of mistake. Nevertheless, granted that absolute being exists, there must be some way in which it contains whatever is positive in contraries and transcends their opposition; otherwise it would split into fragments and could be nothing more than a system of atomic forms such as Plato surmised. The true principle of solution is, no doubt, to recognize absolute being as absolute mind; only mind can contain contraries without contradicting itself. Nicholas does not arrive at this point, but his mathematical puzzles are one kind of stimulus to set out on the way.

At the point at which he does arrive Nicholas remains far from clear, but on his principle of enlightened ignorance he is not surprised at this. Religion evidently demands an affirmative theology, in which we assign positive attributes to God. Men could not be content to worship a pure set of negations. Hence religion speaks of God as wise and good and so forth, but on a more philosophical consideration Nicholas feels constrained to say that a negative theology is nearer the truth. The positive divine attributes seem in the end to be relative to creatures, in so far as God is the source of all wisdom and goodness and the rest. By the way of negation, on the other hand, we are properly denying of God the created characteristics which in himself he does not possess, and thus we are nearer to his real nature (I, 24–6).

Nicholas is now on the edge of an abyss. If the sense in which positive attributes can be assigned to God is exclusively causal and relative to creatures, then we know nothing at all of what God is in himself and even the paradoxical doctrine of the reconciliation of contraries is left without a foundation. This would be genuine agnosticism, but Nicholas stops just in time. For he says that, just as the denial of a greater degree of imperfection to God is more adequate than the denial of a lesser degree, so the affirmation of a greater perfection is nearer the truth than the affirmation of a lesser perfection. Nicholas, as a religious man and a Christian as well as a philosopher, has to make room for an affirmative theology, but he is too afraid of anthropomorphism to go far beyond this bare admission. Here his ignorance is perhaps less than completely enlightened.

By contrast, in the chapters which deal with the doctrine of the Trinity, Nicholas seems to be claiming a kind of insight into its necessity which Christian theologians have not usually supposed themselves to share (I, 7–10, 19–20). The basis of his thought is, as usual, mathematical. Given that unity is first, he holds that equality is logically prior to inequality, since inequality is measured by its distance from equality. Unity, equality, and the identity or connection of unity and equality are in that order the primary notions under which we apprehend the maximum, and it is the same nature of the maximum which is apprehended under them all. Hence the maximum is a trinity in unity, whose members we designate by analogy with created relationships as Father, Son and Holy Spirit. Moreover, it is only a trinity and not a quaternity or any other expression of number, for the triangle is the perfect figure into which all other plane figures can be resolved. It is to be feared that these speculations have little to do with the New Testament doctrine which they profess to illustrate, and we will leave them without further comment.

v

The leading problem of the second book is how the world can be said to be distinct from God. This is obviously a troublesome problem for Nicholas, with his insistence that God is the unity or complication of all reality and that the world is only the explication in limited forms of that same reality, so that the world seems to differ from God only by not-being or nothing. We will not ask whether Nicholas was a pantheist. Pantheism is not a type of philosophical system but a type of philosophical tendency, and all so-called pantheists

xxi

have made some distinction between the absolute and the world of experience. We describe philosophers as pantheists when we judge that their efforts to make an intelligible distinction of this kind have been notably unsuccessful, just as we describe as consumptives those people who have not developed sufficient powers of resistance against the universal germ of tuberculosis. Certainly Nicholas did not think of himself as a pantheist, nor did the generality of his contemporaries think of him in this way. For, although the fifteenth century was one in which accepted philosophical doctrines were on the decline and new speculations were comparatively welcome, there were definite bounds to Christian orthodoxy then as at any other time. No one will find difficulty in agreeing that these bounds excluded pantheism. What we can properly ask about Nicholas is whether the distinction he makes between God and the world is satisfactorily drawn, and our answer may well be that it is in many respects vague and ambiguous although its orthodox intention is equally evident.

Nicholas has no scruple in speaking of God as the supreme universal. *Universale enim penitus absolutum Deus est* (II, 6). The Aristotelians, he thinks, were right in opposing the Platonic theory that the Forms enjoyed an independent reality. They exist only in the mind as universal concepts, but Nicholas pays his due to the Platonists by regarding such a mental existence as higher than and logically prior to their existence in things. Human nature in itself is made neither more nor less by the birth and death of individual human beings. The final implication of this is that everything has its primary reality in the supreme truth which is God. God is the supreme universal, the unity of the possibility of all things in a sense in which possibility is on a higher plane of reality than actual things. This reality is not increased but diminished by the actual existence of things; that is, although it is not diminished in itself, it now exists also in a diminished form. This diminished form of existence can add nothing to the full form in which reality already exists. When we look at creation from the side of God, it seems to be a divine self-limitation; when we look at it from the side of creatures, all their reality seems to be absorbed into God. The world in relation to God has not even as much reality of its own as an accident in relation to a substance (II, 2–3).

God and the world seem to be becoming correlative and inseparable terms. God appears to be for Nicholas simply the creative unity of the possibility of things, the *maximum absolutum* to which the world is related as *maximum contractum*, itself a maximum because the fullest realization of active possibility compatible with the negative and passive possibility inherent in a world of finite things (II, 1). There is no separate world-soul (II, 9), and motion proceeds from the dynamism of the spirit of God (II, 10).

Yet, if Nicholas does not mind speaking of God as the formal cause of the universe, he wants to acknowledge him also as its efficient and final cause (II, 9). The universe is the realization of God's active possibility in a field of passive potentiality which, if it were in itself anything at all, would have to be regarded as opposed to God and which is the source of limitation and defect (II, 8). Thus Nicholas introduces a concept which corresponds with the space of Plato's *Timaeus* and the first matter of Aristotelian physics and which serves to differentiate the world from God. Hence, although God is the absolute entity and quiddity of all things, their contracted or limited entity and quiddity can only be regarded as a reflection and likeness of him (II, 4). In the end there is all the difference between the complete intelligibility and exact truth (*praecisa veritas*) of the divine mode of being and this world of incomplete intelligibility and mere approximation, in which no two things are altogether alike or altogether equal (II, 1). Belonging to this world, we can lay claim only to a knowledge tempered by enlightened ignorance, and it is equally by enlightened ignorance that we glimpse the absolute truth above it.

In summing up the contents of Book II of the *De Docta Ignorantis* we have found ourselves leaping to and fro from one chapter to another and then back to the beginning, and we hope that the reader will charitably suppose that some at least of the obscurity is due to the original text. So many of Nicholas's sentences need to be modified by others which do not always appear in any immediate textual connection with them. The reader would be well advised to proceed rapidly and to form a general impression before puzzling out the exact import of this sentence or of that. Nicholas is eminently an author about whom one must ask what he was trying to say rather than make a spuriously objective grammatical analysis of what he actually did say.

A last note on Book II should point out that on purely metaphysical grounds Nicholas rejected the Aristotelian theory that the earth was at the centre of the universe (II, 11). There can be no centre of the universe, for this would be a point of absolute rest, and such a point is inconceivable in the relative world of creation and would, besides, on the principle of the identity of contraries, coincide with the maximum motion of the circumference. A circumference of the universe is equally unacceptable on its own account, for the world would thus be limited by something and yet there would be nothing beyond it. Hence the world has no centre and no circumference, unless God be described in some sense as both, and everything in the universe is in motion relatively to everything else. This has some interest as showing that the abandonment of Ptolemaic astronomy and Aristotelian physics was in the air at the time, but the argument employed is not of a sort which conduces to the progress of science, and it does not entitle Nicholas to a genuine place among the predecessors of Copernicus and Galileo.

The theme of the third book, which is the Incarnation, is developed in a comparatively straightforward manner. So far Nicholas has considered God in himself and the universe as proceeding from him. The universe is completely dependent upon God but remains in an essential antithesis to him as the limited to the infinite, the relative to the absolute. How is this antithesis to be overcome? How does the creation return to unity with its creator? This is, of course, a time-honoured Neoplatonic theme.

The perfect mode of unity would be a being which was both creator and creature and in which the relative, without ceasing to be relative, would be one with the absolute, *maximum contractum* and *maximum absolutum* at the same time (III, 2). The created being to which this union with God is appropriate would be one which combined all levels of the created world and was thus a miniature universe in itself. But man is such a microcosm combining body and spirit, life, sense and intellect. Hence the crown of creation and the means by which the world returns to its creator would be a human nature in hypostatic union with God (III, 3). It will be seen that Nicholas embraces the thesis of the Scotist school of theologians that the perfection of creation calls in some sense for the Incarnation.

He goes on to show that Christ fulfils this demand (III, 4). Since Christ is both God and man, it is appropriate that he should be born of a human mother by divine intervention without a human father (III, 5). As the head of the human race he pays the debt of death and through death enters into the glory of his resurrection and ascension (III, 6-8). As God made man he is the judge of the human race (III, 9-10). All men must first acknowledge him by faith and then seek to develop that modest understanding which is enlightened ignorance (III, 11). The church is the expression of men's unity with Christ and, through Christ, with God (III, 12). In view of the fissiparous tendencies among Christians in Nicholas's time we can well understand the energy with which he exhorts them to see in the unity of the church the pledge of their unity with Christ. The appeal has not lost its force today.

Any doubts which might have been raised by the first two books about whether Nicholas was a Christian or merely a philosopher are dissipated by the third book. There is no denying that he was a genuine Christian and that he looked on his philosophy, however disconcerting some of it may appear, as an intellectual foundation for an approach to God through Christ. But that is not to say that he was justified in his confidence in it, either as a metaphysical system or as a preamble to Christian theology. The difficult task of evaluating this elusive system must in the last resort be left to the reader, but some suggestions will not be out of place.

VII

Historically Nicholas of Cusa is an interesting and important link between original Neoplatonism, the Neoplatonism of the middle ages and the Platonic systems of the Renaissance. This historical moment is enough to make us judge that he has been unduly neglected. Four editions of his works appeared between the beginning of printing and the Basle volumes of 1565, the third being that prepared by the celebrated Lefèvre of Étaples at Paris in 1514. No further issue of the original text of the *De Docta Ignorantia* was made until Paolo Rotta brought out his edition in 1913. Between the two wars the Heidelberg Academy sought to atone for this neglect by at last producing a fully critical edition of the works, and Henry Bett did something to arouse the attention of the English-speaking public by his excellent monograph, *Nicholas of Cusa* (1932).

But is Nicholas merely an historical curiosity, a predestined

subject for an occasional doctorate thesis? One would like to
know more of the impact which his work made on the men of
his time and of the way in which they understood him. What
might his lively friend Aeneas Sylvius have said about him in
some moment of post-prandial candour? Would Aeneas have
said that he had a bee in his bonnet as far as philosophy was
concerned but that he was such a good fellow and such an
excellent diplomatist that his philosophy had to be indulged?
Or that he was really trying to say much the same as everyone
else but in the obscure manner of those who dwelt north of
the Alps? Or that he was too profound a thinker for many to
understand although he managed to be practical enough in the
affairs of everyday life?

All these statements represent with colloquial simplicity
possible judgments about Nicholas, and none of them is
entirely without justification. A therapeutic positivist could,
no doubt, pick a great deal out of the *De Docta Ignorantia*
which was merely verbiage and had no real significance. Yet
it is surprising how frequently it appears on reflection that
Nicholas is saying in his paradoxical way what any philosophical theist must say and others, perhaps, have expressed less
paradoxically. His theory of the proportional value of human
concepts applied to God is not far from the Thomistic doctrine
of analogy. The joint necessity of the *via positiva* and *via negativa*
is another ancient theme which he works over again, although
with a special emphasis on the side of negation. Enlightened
ignorance is certainly a more suitable and modest characteriza-
tion of the philosophical knowledge of God than would be a
claim to adequately clear and distinct ideas.

Beyond that Nicholas commands respect because he is so
forcibly aware of metaphysical problems as inexhaustible.
Whatever we may be able to say about them, and however true
our statements may be, there is always more to be seen in them
and a more precise answer to be given. The *De Docta Ignorantia*

communicates the sense of mystery without making us recoil into that mere agnosticism which is only another way of evading mystery. Nicholas, struggling to know and to express what he knew, was conscious of how little he knew without doubting that he did know something. The mystery that he acknowledged always remained for him both *mysterium tremendum* and *mysterium fascinans,* and there is implicit in his work the conviction that the end of enlightened ignorance would be more enlightenment rather than irremediable ignorance. If not one of the great philosophers he is at least a genuine and original thinker of considerable power, and no such thinker is wholly without continuing interest.

THE LEARNED IGNORANCE

TO HIS VENERATED MASTER AND
MOST REVEREND FATHER, BELOVED
OF GOD, THE LORD JULIAN, MOST
WORTHY CARDINAL OF THE HOLY
APOSTOLIC SEE

OF GREAT AND WELL-ESTABLISHED INTEL-
lect, you will wonder—and rightly—as to the
meaning of my choosing you as judge and
patron in my too rash attempt to let my crude
ineptitudes see the light. For there can be but little leisure left
to you who, in the discharge of your cardinalitial duties towards the Apostolic See, are so pre-occupied in public affairs
of the greatest moment. It is not, moreover, as if one with your
profound acquaintance with all the Latin writers who have
hitherto acquired fame, as also, now, with Greek writers,
might, by the strangeness of the title be attracted to this probably
quite inept work of mine, since I, with what little ability I may
possess, have already long been very well known to you.

Yet this sense of wonder, arising not so much from your
thinking to find here what was before unknown but rather
from that boldness wherewith I have been led to treat of the
enlightenment of ignorance, will, I hope, attract your enquiring mind, athirst for knowledge. Physiologists, we know, say
that a kind of unpleasant sensation in the stomach precedes
appetite, that thereby nature in her attempt at self-conservation

3

may be stimulated and refreshed. It is thus, I rightly deem, a subject for wonder, and accordingly a subject for philosophizing upon, that there pre-exists a craving for knowledge in order that the intellect, whose being is in understanding, may be perfected by the study of truth. Rare things, especially if they are curious, are wont to excite our interest. On these grounds, therefore, peerless teacher, deign in your kindness to think that something of worth may here lie hidden, and accept from a German a method of reasoning in divine things which, whatever it may be like, the considerable toil involved has rendered most pleasing to me.

THE FIRST BOOK

CHAPTER I. HOW KNOWLEDGE IS IGNORANCE

WE SEE THAT GOD HAS IMPLANTED IN all things a natural desire to exist with the fullest measure of existence that is compatible with their particular nature. To this end they are endowed with suitable faculties and activities; and by means of these there is in them a discernment that is natural and in keeping with the purpose of their knowledge, which ensures their natural inclination serving its purpose and being able to reach its fulfilment in that object towards which it is attracted by the weight of its own nature. If at times this does not happen, it is necessarily the result of an accident, as when sickness deceives taste or conjecture upsets calculation. That is the explanation of the sound untrammelled intellect's desire for truth, which, by its natural discursive movement, it ceaselessly seeks in all things; and once it takes possession of the object of its natural desire, we say it knows the truth; for, without any hesitation, we call that true, which no sound mind can refuse to embrace. In every enquiry men judge of the uncertain by comparing it with an object presupposed certain, and their judgment is always approximative; every enquiry is, therefore, comparative and uses the method of analogy. When there is comparatively little distance from the object of enquiry back to the object regarded as certain, a judgment is easily formed; when many intermediaries are required, the task becomes difficult. We are familiar enough with this in mathematics, in which the reducing of the first propositions to the well-known first principles is easier, whereas the more remote propositions give rise to more difficulty, because it is only by means of the first propositions that these can be led back to the first principles. Every enquiry, therefore, consists in a relation of comparison that is easy or difficult to draw; for this reason the infinite as infinite is unknown, since it is away and above all comparison. Now, while proportion expresses an agreement in some one thing, it expresses at the same time a distinction, so that it cannot be understood without number. Number, in consequence, includes all things that are capable of comparison. It is not then in quantity only that number produces proportion; it produces it in all things that are capable of agreement and difference in any way at all, whether substantially or accidentally. That is why Pythagoras was so insistent on maintaining that in virtue of numbers all things were understood.

It so far surpasses human reason, however, to know the precision of the combinations in material things and how exactly the known has to be adapted to the unknown that Socrates thought he knew nothing save his own ignorance, whilst Solomon, the Wise, affirmed that in all things there are difficulties which beggar explanation in words; and we have it from another, who was divinely inspired, that wisdom and the locality of the understanding lie hidden from the eyes of all the living. If this is so—and even the most profound Aristotle in his First Philosophy affirms it to be true of the things most evident to us in nature—then in presence of such difficulty we may be compared to owls trying to look at the sun; but since the natural desire in us for knowledge is not without a purpose, its immediate object is our own ignorance. If we can fully realize this desire, we will acquire learned ignorance. Nothing could be more beneficial for even the most zealous searcher for knowledge than his being in fact most learned in that very ignorance which is peculiarly his own; and the better a man will have known his own ignorance, the greater his learning will be. It is in bearing this in mind that I have undertaken the task of writing a few words on learned ignorance.

CHAPTER II. PRELIMINARY EXPLAN-ATION OF ALL THAT FOLLOWS

AS I AM ABOUT TO DEAL WITH IGNORANCE AS THE greatest learning, I consider it necessary to determine the precise meaning of the maximum or greatest. We speak of a thing being the greatest or maximum when nothing greater than it can exist. But to one being alone does plenitude belong, with the result that unity, which is also being, and the maximum are identical; for if such a unity is itself in every way and entirely without restriction then it is clear that there is nothing to be placed in opposition to it, since it is the absolute maximum. Consequently, the absolute maximum is one and it is all; all things are in it because it is the maximum. Moreover, it is in all things for this reason that the minimum at once coincides with it, since there is nothing that can be placed in opposition to it. Because it is absolute, it is in actuality all possible being, limiting all things and receiving no limitation from any. In the First Book I will endeavour to study this maximum, who without any doubt is believed to be the God of all nations. It is a study that is above reason and cannot be conducted on the lines of human comprehension; and for my guide I will take him alone who dwells in light inaccessible.

In the second place, just as we have the absolute maximum, which is the absolute entity by which all things are what they are, so we have from it the universal unity of being which is called the maximum effect of the absolute. In consequence, its existence as the universe is finite, and its unity, which could not be absolute, is the relative unity of a plurality. Though this maximum embraces all things in its universal unity, so that all that comes from the absolute is in it and it in all, yet it could not subsist outside the plurality in which it is contained, for this restriction is inseparably bound up with its existence. Of this maximum, which is the universe, I will have something further to say in the second book.

In the third place, we shall see that there is still one more manner in which to consider the maximum. Since the subsistence in plurality of the universe is necessarily finite, we shall study the plurality itself of things in order to discover the one maximum in which the universe finds especially and most completely its actual and ultimate subsistence. This maximum in the universe is united with the absolute, for the absolute is the ultimate term of all; and as this maximum, which is at once relative and absolute, is the most perfect realization of the purpose of the universe and entirely beyond our reach, my comments on it will be added in accordance with the inspiration of Jesus himself; in fact, this maximum bears the ever blessed name of Jesus.

An understanding of this matter will be attained rather by our rising above the literal sense of the words, than by insisting upon their natural properties, for these natural properties cannot be effectively adapted to such intellectual mysteries. For the reader we must even use drawings as illustrations, but he must rise above these in leaving aside what is sensible in them in order to arrive unimpeded at what is purely intelligible. In pursuing this method I have eagerly tried, by the avoidance of all difficulties of expressions, to make it as clear as possible to the average mind that the foundation for learned ignorance is the fact that absolute truth is beyond our grasp.

CHAPTER III. ABSOLUTE TRUTH IS BEYOND OUR GRASP

FROM THE SELF-EVIDENT FACT THAT THERE IS NO gradation from infinite to finite, it is clear that the simple maximum is not to be found where we meet degrees of more and less; for such degrees are finite, whereas the simple maximum is necessarily infinite. It is manifest, therefore, that when anything other than the simple maximum itself is given, it will always be possible to find something greater. Equality, we find, is a matter of degree: with things that are alike one is more equal to this than to that, in-so-far as they belong, or do not belong, to the same genus or species, or in-so-far as they are, or are not, related in time, place or influence. For that reason it is evident that two or more things cannot be so alike and equal that an infinite number of similar objects cannot still be found. No matter, then, how equal the measure and the thing measured are, they will remain for ever different.

A finite intellect, therefore, cannot by means of comparison reach the absolute truth of things. Being by nature indivisible, truth excludes 'more' or 'less', so that nothing but truth itself can be the exact measure of truth: for instance, that which is not a circle cannot be the measure of a circle, for the nature of a circle is one and indivisible. In consequence, our intellect, which is not the truth, never grasps the truth with such precision that it could not be comprehended with infinitely greater precision. The relationship of our intellect to the truth is like that of a polygon to a circle; the resemblance to the circle grows with the multiplication of the angles of the polygon; but apart from its being reduced to identity with the circle, no multiplication, even if it were infinite, of its angles will make the polygon equal the circle.

11

It is clear, therefore, that all we know of the truth is that the absolute truth, such as it is, is beyond our reach. The truth, which can be neither more nor less than it is, is the most absolute necessity, while, in contrast with it, our intellect is possibility. Therefore, the quiddity of things, which is onto-logical truth, is unattainable in its entirety; and though it has been the objective of all philosophers, by none has it been found as it really is. The more profoundly we learn this lesson of ignorance, the closer we draw to truth itself.

CHAPTER IV. THE ABSOLUTE MAXI-MUM IS KNOWN BUT NOT UNDER-STOOD. MAXIMUM AND MINIMUM ARE SYNONYMOUS

THERE CAN BE NOTHING GREATER IN EXISTENCE than the simple, absolute maximum; and since it is greater than our powers of comprehension—for it is infinite truth—our knowledge of it can never mean that we comprehend it. It is above all that we can conceive, for its nature excludes degrees of 'more' and 'less'. All the things, in fact, that we apprehend by our senses, reason or intellect are so different from one another that there is no precise equality between them. The maximum equality, therefore, in which there is no diversity or difference from any other, is completely beyond our understanding; and for that reason the absolute maximum is in act most perfect, since it is in act all that it can be. Being all that it can be, it is, for one and the same reason, as great as it can be and as small as it can be. By definition the minimum is that which cannot be less than it is; and since that is also true of the maximum, it is evident that the minimum is identified with the maximum.

This becomes clearer when you restrict your considerations to the maximum and the minimum of quantity. The maximum quantity is infinitely great, whilst the minimum is infinitely small. Now, if mentally you lay aside the notions of greatness and smallness, you are left with the maximum and the minimum without quantity, and it becomes clear that the maximum and the minimum are one and the same; in fact, the minimum is as much a superlative as the maximum. The maximum and the minimum, then, are equally predicable of absolute quantity, since in it they are identified.

Distinctions, therefore, are only found to exist among things which are susceptible of 'more' and 'less'; and they exist among these in different ways; in no way do they exist in the absolute maximum, for it is above any form of affirmation and negation. Existence and non-existence can be equally predicated of all that which is conceived to exist; and non-existence cannot to any greater degree than existence be affirmed of all that is conceived not to exist. But the absolute maximum, in consequence, is all things and, whilst being all, it is none of them; in other words, it is at once the maximum and minimum of being. There is, in fact, no difference between these two affirmations: 'God, who is the absolute maximum itself, is light'; and 'God is light at its highest, therefore He is light at its lowest'. It could not be otherwise; for the absolute maximum would not be the realization of all possible perfection, if it were not infinite and if it were not the end to which all things are ordained, whilst it stands subordinate to none. With God's help, we shall explain this in the pages that follow.

This is far and away beyond our understanding, which is fundamentally unable by any rational process to reconcile contradictories. We proceed to truth through the things made known to us by nature; and, as this process falls very far short of the infinite power of the maximum, we are unable to link together by means of it contradictories which are infinitely distant from one another. We know that the absolute maximum is infinite, that it is all things since it is one with the minimum; but this knowledge is away and above any understanding we could reach by discursive reasoning. In this book the terms maximum and minimum are not restricted to quantity of mass or of force; they have here an absolutely transcendent value embracing all things in their absolute simplicity.

CHAPTER V. ONENESS OF THE MAXIMUM

IN WHAT FOLLOWS WE WILL GIVE A STILL CLEARER explanation of what must now be very evident from the foregoing, namely that the absolute maximum is beyond our comprehension yet intelligible, able to be named whilst remaining ineffable. The discursive reason gives names only to those things which are susceptible of 'more' or 'less'; when confronted with the greatest possible or the smallest possible, it is unable to find a name for it. The fact that all things have existence in the best possible way makes it impossible to have plurality of beings without number; for if number is denied then the distinction, hierarchy, relationship, harmony and even plurality of beings must be denied. We would be forced to the same conclusions if the number were infinite, for in that case it would be the maximum in actuality which would be one with the minimum: it is one and the same thing to call a number infinite and to say it is the minimum. If, then, by numerical addition we were to arrive at an actual maximum, since number is finite, we would not have thereby reached the maximum which is the greatest possible, since this would be infinite. Clearly, then, numerical addition is actually finite and will be capable of receiving one more. In the opposite direction the

14

same holds good: just as a higher number is always possible by addition, so no matter how small the given number actually is, a smaller will always be possible by subtraction. If that were not true, number would not be the key to the distinction of thing from thing, nor of the hierarchy of beings; and we could not speak of things in the plural, nor of a 'more' or 'less'; number itself, besides, could not exist. We must in consequence reach a minimum in number which is the smallest possible. Unity is such a minimum; and as there can be nothing less than it, unity will be the simple (absolute) minimum that coincides, as we have just seen, with the maximum.

Being capable of being added to, number can by no means be the simple minimum or maximum; unity cannot, therefore, be a number, though as minimum it is the principle of all number. Therefore absolute unity, where no duality is possible, is the absolute maximum or God Himself. By the fact that it is unity at its absolute perfection, it excludes the possibility of the existence of another such being because it is all that it can be. It cannot therefore, be a number.

Number has led us to the conclusion that absolute unity is a most fitting attribute of God, the ineffable, and that His unity is such that He is actually all that is possible. His is a unity which excludes degrees of 'more' or 'less' and even the possible existence of another being of the same order. God, in consequence, is infinite unity. Nothing could be truer than his own words: 'Hear, O Israel: the Lord our God is one Lord'; and 'For one is your master . . . one is your father, who is in heaven'; nothing could be more false than the assertion that there is more than one God, for it is nothing short of a denial of God and the entire universe, as we shall prove later. Number, a being of reason, owes its existence to our power of comparing and distinguishing; its reality is limited to the reality it has in my mind; number, therefore, could not exist if it were not taken for granted that it necessarily proceeds from unity. Clearly, too, the multiplicity of beings that proceed from this infinite unity, are so really dependent upon it that without it they could not exist. How could they exist without being? Absolute Unity is infinite being, as we shall see later.

CHAPTER VI. THE MAXIMUM IS ABSOLUTE NECESSITY

FROM WHAT HAS BEEN SAID IT MUST NOW BE CLEAR that the absolute maximum alone is infinite and that all else, in reference to it, is finite and limited. Finite, limited being has a beginning and an end, so that there is a being to which it owes existence and in which it will have its end. It would be erroneous to say that that being, finite itself, was greater than any given finite being; equally erroneous would it be to say that we arrive at such a being through an infinite series of greater and greater finite beings; for, in the first place, an actual, infinite series of finites is impossible and, secondly, such a maximum would itself be finite. Therefore, the beginning and end of all finite things is necessarily the Absolute Maximum.

Besides, if the Absolute Maximum did not exist, nothing could be; for all beings less than the Maximum are finite; necessarily they are effects that are produced by another. To say that they produced themselves would be the same as saying that they acted before they existed; to explain them by appealing to an infinite number of principles and causes has been already ruled out. That will be the Absolute Maximum, without which nothing is able to be.

Moreover, supposing the maximum reduced to being, we may say: Nothing is in opposition to the maximum; and for that reason both non-being and minimum being are identical with the maximum. How, then, is it possible to conceive the maximum as incapable of existence, since minimum being is maximum being? Without being we can have no idea that anything exists. But absolute being necessarily is the absolute maximum; therefore, nothing can be conceived to exist independently of the maximum.

Maximum truth, besides, is the absolute maximum. All that we can say or think is exhausted by the following propositions which are the maximum truth on the absolute maximum itself: it is or it is not; it is and it is not; it neither is nor is it not. My point is made no matter which of these you affirm as truth at its maximum, for in the simple maximum I have the maximum truth.

From the foregoing it is clear that 'being' or any other word is not the precise name of the maximum; it is above every name; yet the name 'maximum', must mean that being in the highest, though indescribable, way is predicated of it more than of any being that can be described. For these and a host of similar reasons the ignorance that is learning understands most clearly that the absolute maximum so necessarily exists that it is absolute necessity. Now it has been established that there can be only one absolute maximum; this unity, therefore, of the maximum is the greatest truth.

CHAPTER VII. ETERNAL UNITY AND TRINITY

NO NATION EVER EXISTED WHICH DID NOT WORSHIP God and believe that He was the absolute maximum. We find that Marcus Varro, in his *Antiquities*, has drawn attention to the fact that the 'Sissennii' adored the Unity as the maximum, while Pythagoras, whose authority in his day was beyond dispute, maintained that that unity was a trinity. If we give our minds more deeply to the study of the truth of this contention of Pythagoras, we may argue thus according to our premises: That which precedes all diversity is undoubtedly eternal; for diversity and changeableness are the same thing; but all that naturally precedes changeableness is unchangeable, therefore eternal. As it takes two to make a diversity, diversity like number is posterior to unity. By nature, therefore, unity is prior to diversity, and, by reason of this natural priority, unity is eternal.

All inequality, moreover, arises from an equality plus something: inequality, therefore, is by nature posterior to equality, and this by reduction can be most convincingly established. All inequality is reduced to an equality, for the equal lies between the greater and the lesser. If, then, we remove that which is in excess, equality will be established: if, on the other hand, we have to deal with the lesser, we will establish equality by removing from the other that which is in excess. We can go on with this process of removal until we come to the simple elements. It is evident, then, that all inequality is in this way reducible to equality. Therefore, equality naturally precedes inequality.

But inequality and diversity are by nature simultaneous: where there is inequality, there is necessarily diversity, and conversely. Where, in fact, there are at least two things, there will be diversity, and, because there is duplication, there will be inequality. It is particularly, therefore, because duality constitutes the first diversity and the first inequality, that inequality will naturally exist where there is diversity. Having proved that equality is by nature prior to inequality, we have thereby established that it is also naturally prior to diversity. Equality, it must be concluded, is eternal.

Further, if one of two causes is by nature prior to the other, then the effect of the first will be by nature prior to the effect of the second. Now unity is either the cause of the connection or it is the connection itself: and that is why we say that things are connected when they are united. Duality, on the other hand, is either the cause of division or it is itself division, for duality is the first division. As unity, then, is the cause of connection and duality the cause of division, it logically follows that just as unity is by nature prior to duality, so connection is prior naturally to division. Now division and diversity are by nature always found together; we conclude, on that account, that since connection is prior by nature to diversity, it must like unity be eternal.

Our proof has been that, because unity is eternal, and equality eternal, the connection is likewise eternal. But it is impossible for several eternals to exist; if several were to exist, then, because unity precedes all plurality, there would exist something which would be prior by nature to eternity, which is absurd. Besides, if there were several eternal beings, one would possess something which another lacked and so none of them would be perfect; in other words, there would exist an eternal which was not eternal at all, since it is imperfect. This absurdity manifests the impossibility of several eternals. We are left with the conclusion that unity, equality and connection, which are equally eternal, are one. That is the unity which is at once a trinity that Pythagoras—the first of philosophers and the honour of Italy and Greece—held up for adoration.

We will now go on to give a more detailed explanation of the generation of equality from unity.

CHAPTER VIII. ETERNAL GENERATION

IN A FEW WORDS WE WILL NOW SHOW HOW EQUALITY of unity is born from unity, and how the connection proceeds from unity and the equality of unity.

From the Greek word, 'ὤν', which gives us 'ens' in Latin, we get unity—'ὤντας', so to speak. Unity and entity may be regarded as convertible, for God is entity; He is the intrinsic principle of essence and for that reason is the very entity of things. Equality of entity—or the uniformity of essence or existence, which is the same thing—may be taken to be convertible with equality of unity. Where the essence is uniform, there can be no room in a thing for degrees of more or less, no question of above, or beneath; for if a thing has more than the essence demands, it would be a monster if, on the other hand, it has less, it could not be regarded as equal or uniform in essence.

The study of the nature of generation enables us to form a clear notion of this generation of equality from unity. Generation is, in fact, either the multiplication of the same nature proceeding from the father to the son or the repetition of unity. Where unity is multiplied twice, three times or oftener, this form of generation is peculiar to things finite; where, on the contrary, we have unity not twice multiplied but unity once, or a solitary repetition of unity, we have the generation of unity from unity; this kind of generation is eternal. It engenders equality of unity, which can be conceived solely by the generation of unity by unity.

CHAPTER IX. ETERNAL PROCESSION OF THE CONNECTION

JUST AS THE GENERATION OF UNITY FROM UNITY IS A single repetition of unity, so the procession from both is a repetition of this repetition of unity; or, if you will, it is the uniting of unity and the equality of unity itself. Procession is regarded as a sort of extension from the one to the other; e.g. when two things are equal, they are connected and united in some sort of way by the equality which extends, so to speak, from one to the other. It is correct, consequently, to say that the connection proceeds from unity and from the equality of unity, for there can be no connection of one by itself. Since unity proceeds from unity to equality and from equality of unity to unity, since it is, as it were, an extension of the one to the other, it is rightly said to proceed from both. Our reason for not having said that the connection is generated either by unity or the equality of unity is that the connection does not owe its existence to a repetition or a multiplication of unity. None the less, unity, the equality of unity and the connection proceeding from both are one and the same, though the equality of unity is engendered by unity and the connection proceeds from both; it is as if we were to use the words, 'hoc', 'id', 'idem' in reference to one and the same thing. What we have named 'id' is related to the first and what we have called 'idem' connects and unites the related (being) to the first. If from the pronoun 'id' we coined the word 'iditas', we should then be able to use the terms, 'unitas', 'iditas', 'identitas', which in their application to the Trinity would not be inadmissible; 'iditas' would constitute the relation to unity, whilst 'identitas' would denote the connection of 'iditas' and unity.

It was a comparison drawn from things finite that led our

saintly doctors to call the Father Unity, the Son Equality, and the Holy Ghost Connection. As it is one and the same nature which father and son have in common, the son is in nature the equal of the father, for the human nature in both of them does not differ in the slightest degree, and between them there exists a certain connection. By the very fact that they share the same nature, they are joined to one another by the bond of natural love; and the father loves his son in preference to all other men because it is from him that human nature comes to the son.

It was from such a most distant resemblance that the name, Unity was given to the Father, Equality to the Son and Connection or Love to the Holy Ghost—names that have reference only to creatures, as we shall see more clearly later, when we deal specifically with the question. Following, therefore, the Pythagorean method of enquiry, we have here, in my opinion, a most revealing examination of the ever-adorable Trinity in Unity and Unity in Trinity.

CHAPTER X. HOW THE UNDERSTANDING OF THE TRINITY IN UNITY TRANSCENDS ALL THINGS

WE MAY NOW EXAMINE WHAT MARTIAN MEANS when he says that Philosophy has ejected circles and spheres in attempting to attain a knowledge of this Trinity.

We have previously shown that there is only one Maximum and that it is absolutely simple; that no figure is such, neither the most perfect solid (like the sphere), nor plane (like the circle), nor rectilinear (like the triangle); nor is the simple straight line such a Maximum. It is so far away and above all these that we are compelled to eject all that the senses or imagination or reason with its material accretions can give us, if we would reach this absolutely simple and abstract intelligence, where all things are one; where the line is a triangle, circle and sphere; where unity is trinity and trinity, unity; where accident is substance, body, spirit; movement, rest and so on. We have a correct notion of unity only when we have grasped that each thing is in Unity, that Unity itself is all things and that, in consequence, each thing in unity is all things. If we do not understand that the Maximum Unity itself must be a Trinity, it is because we have not duly ejected the sphere, circle and the rest; for there is one way and only one way of correctly understanding the Supreme Unity and that is as a Trinity.

Let us point this truth with apt illustrations. It is evident that in the unity of the understanding there is necessarily the intelligent being, the intelligible object and the act of understanding. Suppose, now, you want to pass from intelligent being to the Absolute Intelligent Being, you would say that the Absolute is the absolutely Supreme Intelligent Being; unless you were to add that He is also the absolutely Supreme Intelligible and the absolutely Supreme Act of Understanding, you would not have a correct idea of the absolute and most perfect Unity. For if Unity is understanding at its highest and most perfect, and if understanding necessarily supposes the three co-relationships—intelligent being, intelligible object and act of understanding, then it follows that the correct concept of Unity must be of three in one.

Unity, in fact, is a trinity, for unity means non-division, distinction and connection or union. These three—non-division, distinction and connection—have their origin in unity; necessarily, then, the Absolute Unity will be non-division, distinction and connection. Just as the eternal is that which is not separated from anything, so the Absolute Unity had no beginning or is eternity, because it is non-division (in the Absolute); it is from an immutable eternity, because it is distinction; and it proceeds from both (non-division and distinction), because it is connection or union.

Further, when I say that 'Unity is the maximum', I am calling it a trinity; in fact when I speak of unity, I am speaking of a beginning that had no beginning; when I use the word maximum I am referring to a beginning from a principle; when I join and unite these by the verb 'to be', I am speaking of a procession from both. It has already been most clearly established that the maximum is one, for the minimum, maximum and connection are one; unity itself is the minimum, the maximum and the connection; if that is so, it becomes evident that a philosophy which would understand the necessity of the maximum unity's being a trinity could only do so by means of a simple intuition, for no help that the imagination and reason can lend would be of any avail here.

Such statements as these: 'He who would grasp the maximum in a simple intuition must rise above the differences and diversities of things and above all mathematical figures', and 'The line in the maximum is a surface and a circle and a sphere' will have caused you much surprise. That I may the more easily, then, enable your intellect to penetrate and grasp the necessity and truth of these statements, I will make use of an example that is beyond all doubt; if, by a correct interpretation of that example, you reach the truth and understand these statements, you will duly experience a wondrous delight; for you will advance in learned ignorance in this way and will come to grasp, as well as any human intellect can, that the one incomprehensible Absolute is the ever-blessed, triune God.

CHAPTER XI. MATHEMATICS ARE A VERY GREAT HELP IN THE UNDERSTANDING OF DIFFERENT DIVINE TRUTHS

ALL OUR GREATEST PHILOSOPHERS AND THEOlogians unanimously assert that the visible universe is a faithful reflection of the invisible, and that from creatures we can rise to a knowledge of the Creator, 'in a mirror and in a dark manner', as it were. The fundamental reason for the use of symbolism in the study of spiritual things, which in themselves are beyond our reach, has already been given. Though we neither perceive it nor understand it, we know for a fact that all things stand in some sort of relation to one another; that, in virtue of this inter-relation, all the individuals constitute one universe and that in the one Absolute the multiplicity of beings is unity itself. Every image is an approximate reproduction of the exemplar; yet, apart from the Absolute image or the Exemplar itself in unity of nature, no image will so faithfully or precisely reproduce the exemplar, as to rule out the possibility of an infinity of more faithful and precise images, as we have already made clear.

When we use an image and try to reach analogically what is as yet unknown, there must be no doubt at all about the image; for it is only by way of postulates and things certain that we can arrive at the unknown. But in all things sensible material possibility abounds which explains their being in a continual state of flux. Our knowledge of things is not acquired by completely disregarding their material conditions, without which no image of them could be formed; nor is it wholly subject to their possible variations; but the more we abstract from sensible conditions, the more certain and solid our knowledge is.

Mathematics is an example of such abstract knowledge. That explains why philosophers so readily turned to mathematics for examples of the things which the intellect had to investigate; and none of the masters of old, when solving a difficulty, used other than mathematical illustrations, so that Boethius, the most learned of Romans, went so far as to say that knowledge of things divine was impossible without some knowledge of mathematics.

Was not the key to all truth to be found in numbers, according to Pythagoras, who was the first to be called a philosopher and who was the first philosopher in fact? In so far as they have followed him, the Platonists and the chief of our own philosophers, like Augustine and later Boethius, have not hesitated to assert that number was the essential exemplar in the mind of the Creator of all things to be created. Aristotle, who, by disagreeing with the Platonists, seemed to desire to be an exception to the rule, found it impossible in his Metaphysics to explain the specific differences otherwise than by a comparison with numbers; and when he wishes to show that in nature one form is in another, he is forced to turn to mathematical figures for an illustration: 'Just as the triangle is in the tetragon, so is the lower form contained in the higher'; and he has innumerable examples of this kind that there is no need to mention. It was also to mathematics that Aurelius Augustine, the Platonist, turned for assistance in dealing with such questions as the quantity of the soul and its immortality and other lofty subjects. Boethius had such high regard for this method that he constantly affirmed that all truth was contained in numbers and magnitude. And if you would have me be more concise,— was it not solely by the mathematical demonstration of the Pythagoreans and the Peripatetics that the Epicureans' teaching about the atoms in the void was refuted—a teaching that at once involved the denial of God's existence and the collapse of all truth? And the principle taken for granted by Epicurus was that there could be found ultimately in all things simple indivisible atoms.

Following in the way of the Ancients, we are in complete agreement with them in saying that, since there is no other approach to a knowledge of things divine than that of symbols, we cannot do better than use mathematical signs on account of their indestructible certitude.

CHAPTER XII. THE WAY IN WHICH MATHEMATICAL SIGNS SHOULD BE USED FOR OUR PURPOSE

IT IS NOW EVIDENT FROM WHAT WE HAVE SAID THAT no object that we know or of which we have any idea, can be the Absolute Maximum; and since it is by way of symbols that we intend to conduct our search of it, we must, therefore, look for something more than a simple comparison. In mathematics, in fact, we are always dealing with finite things, for if they were not finite we could form no idea of them at all. If then we want to reach the Absolute Maximum through the finite, we must, in the first place, study finite, mathematical figures as they are, namely a mixture of potency and act; then we must attribute the respective perfections to the corresponding infinite figures, and finally we must, in a much more sublime way, attribute the perfections of the infinite figures to the simple Infinite, which cannot possibly be expressed by any figure. Then, whilst we are groping in the dark, our ignorance will enlighten us in an incomprehensible fashion and enable us to form a more correct and truer notion of the Absolute.

By this method, and guided by Infinite Truth, we note the difference of expressions used by saintly men and brilliant intellects who gave themselves to the study of figures. St. Anselm, for instance, compared Absolute Truth to infinite straightness; following him, we will take the straight line as our figure of straightness. Some very learned men have drawn a comparison between the Most Holy Trinity and a triangle whose three angles are right angles; such a triangle could be called infinite, since its sides, as we shall see, must be infinite; we will also follow this opinion. Others, striving to depict the infinite unity, have said God is an infinite circle; and there are those who have likened God to an infinite sphere from their considerations of His most perfect act of existence. We shall show that all these views are correct and that they all form only one opinion.

CHAPTER XIII. MODIFICATIONS OF THE ABSOLUTE INFINITE LINE

IF THERE WERE AN INFINITE LINE, I MAINTAIN THAT it would be at once a straight line, a triangle, a circle, a sphere; similarly, if there were an infinite sphere, it would at once be a circle, a triangle and a line; and it would be likewise with the infinite triangle and infinite circle.

In the first place, it is evident that the infinite line would be a straight line. The diameter of a circle is a straight line; the circumference is a curved line and longer than the diameter. Now, if the curve of the circumference becomes less curved as the circle expands, the circumference of the absolutely greatest possible circle will be the smallest possible curve; it will be, therefore, absolutely straight. The maximum and the minimum are, therefore, so identified that we most clearly perceive that in the infinite there is the absolute maximum of straightness with the absolute minimum of curve. A study of the figure here given will dispel all possible doubt on this point. We see that the arc C–D of the larger circle is less curved than the arc E–F of the smaller circle, and that E–F is itself less curved than the arc G–H of a still smaller circle; the straight line A–B will, therefore, be the arc of the greatest possible circle.

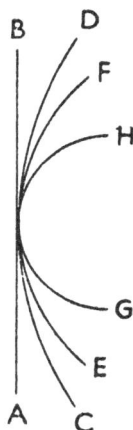

In this our first point is proved, for we have shown that the simply infinite line is, of necessity, perfectly straight, and that in such a line straightness and curve are not mutually exclusive but are one and the same thing.

We have said, secondly, that the infinite line is an infinite triangle, circle or sphere. To establish this we must discover from a study of finite lines the potentiality of the finite line; we shall bring out more clearly from this the point we are trying to make, since we know that all that is potential in a finite line is actual in an infinite line.

Now we know that a finite line is never so long or so straight that it cannot be longer or straighter, and it has already been proved that the infinite line is the longest and straightest. If then we have a line A–B, and if while the point 'A' remains fixed, the line is moved till it reaches C, a triangle is described; if the movement of that line is continued till it returns to B, a circle is described. With 'A' still fixed, let us suppose B is again moved till it reaches D which is directly opposite the initial point B; A–B and A–D form one continuous line and a semicircle is described. Let us suppose next that the diameter B–D is fixed and that the semicircle is turned completely round; we have then a sphere, and the sphere is the ultimate and total actualization of a line, for no more perfect figure is able to be produced from the sphere.

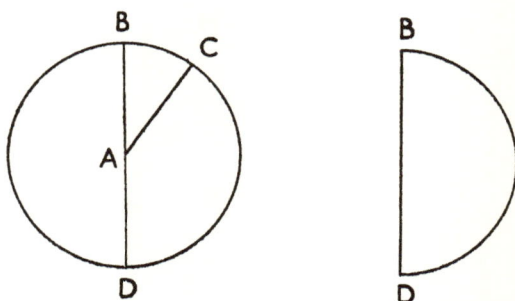

If, therefore, the finite line is potentially all the above figures and if in the infinite line all the potentialities of the finite line are actualized, then it follows that the infinite line is a triangle, a circle and a sphere; and that is what had to be proved.

If you would like a clearer explanation of how the potentialities of the finite are actualised in the infinite, I shall completely convince you.

CHAPTER XIV. THE INFINITE LINE IS A TRIANGLE

To the imagination the coincidence of the straight line and a triangle will always seem an impossibility, for in scope the imagination is limited to the material order and there could never be anything but disproportion between a material line and a triangle; but for the intellect it is not difficult to grasp that a line can be a triangle. We have, in fact, already established that there can be but one Absolute and Infinite. Now, since any two sides of a triangle when joined cannot be smaller than the third, it is evident that in a triangle which has one side infinite the others cannot be smaller. As every part of the infinite is infinite, it necessarily follows that, if one side of a triangle is infinite, the others are equally infinite. It is impossible to have more than one infinite; therefore, our transcendental conclusion is that the infinite triangle, though it is the perfect model of all triangles, is not composed of a plurality of lines, is not in any sense a compound, but is most perfectly indivisible; and since it is the perfect model triangle, it must have three lines; therefore, the one infinite line is itself three lines and these three lines are one perfectly indivisible line. The same holds good from the angles and the three are one. And that infinite triangle will not be composed of sides and angles; the infinite line and angle are one and the same thing, so that the line is the angle, because the triangle is the line.

You will also find it helpful in the grasping of this truth, if, instead of restricting your study to a triangle of the sensible order, you go on to consider the ideal triangle. In every triangle of the sensible order the angles are equal to two right angles; the greater one angle is, the proportionately smaller are the others. According to our first principle, the limit to the possible expansion of any one angle is less than 180°, but if we suppose that the angle is fully extended to 180°, without the triangle's ceasing to exist, then it is evident that it is a triangle of one angle which is three, and that the three are one.

Similarly you can see how a triangle is a line. Any two lines of a triangle in the sensible order, when joined together, are greater than the third line, the more the angle they form becomes acute; e.g. the lines B-A and A-C when joined together are much longer than B–C, because the angle B–A–C, is more acute. Inversely, the greater the angle, B–D–C, for example, the less B–D and D–C when joined exceed B–C in length, and the smaller the surface is. If, then, we were to suppose that the angle were one of 180°, the entire triangle would be reduced to a simple line.

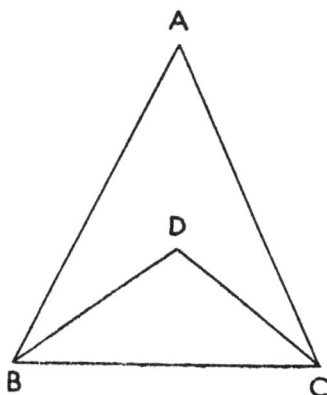

In consequence, this supposition, though unrealizable in the material order, can assist you in your mounting to the intelligible order, where what is impossible in the material order is seen not only as a possibility but as an absolute necessity; there it is evident that the infinite line is the infinite triangle; and this is what we undertook to show.

CHAPTER XV. THE INFINITE TRIANGLE IS A CIRCLE AND A SPHERE

WE CAN SEE NOW MORE CLEARLY HOW THE triangle is a circle. Let us suppose that the triangle A–B–C is described by the line A–B moving from the fixed point A until it falls on C; were the line infinite and were it to continue its revolution till it returned to its initial position, there is no doubt we would have the infinite circle of which B–C is a part. Being a part of an infinite arc, B–C is then a straight line. Now as every part of the infinite is infinite, therefore B–C is not smaller than the entire, infinite circumference; B–C, therefore, is not only a part but is, in the fullest sense, the circumference. Necessarily we must conclude that the triangle A–B–C is the infinite circle.

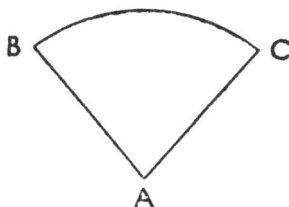

Since the circumference B–C is a straight line and infinite, A–B cannot be greater than it, for there is nothing greater than infinity; in fact, they are not two distinct lines, for it is impossible to have two infinities. The infinite line, therefore, which is a triangle is also a circle, and this we set out to prove.

In this way it can be shown very clearly that the infinite line is also a sphere; the line A–B, we have already proved, is not only the circumference of the infinite circle but is even the circle itself; and, as we said, in describing the triangle it moved till B fell on C. Now it has also been proved that B–C is an infinite line, therefore A–B returns to C by a complete revolution on its own axis; and when a circle revolves in this way, it necessarily generates a sphere. If, then, as we have proved, A–B–C is a circle, a triangle and a line, we have now the proof that it is also a sphere. These are in fact the truths we set out to examine.

CHAPTER XVI. THE RELATIONSHIP OF THE MAXIMUM TO ALL THINGS IS BY ANALOGY WHAT THE INFINITE LINE IS TO LINES

NOW THAT WE KNOW HOW THE INFINITE LINE IS the infinite actualization of all that is potential in the finite line, we know by analogy how, in the simple Maximum, in a similar way, the Maximum itself is the infinite actualization of all that is simply and absolutely possible. For the Maximum is the infinite, actual existence of all that is possible—the infinite, actual existence, we must note, and not merely the finite realization of what is possible. An example will illustrate our meaning: a triangle is educed from a line; the infinite line is not that triangle such as is educed from the finite line; the infinite line is the actually existing infinite triangle; they are one and the same. Further, just as the infinite line is the sphere actually existing, so in the Maximum absolute possibility itself and infinite actual existence are perfectly identified. In the finite order this is not so, for there potency is not act, a finite line is not a triangle.

We now see what great truths can be deduced from this about the Maximum, how its nature is such that in it the minimum is the Maximum, so that it is infinitely all without any distinction. From this principle it is possible to deduce all the negative truths on the Maximum that are able to be formulated; in fact, even all the theology we are capable of learning comes from this great principle. It was for that reason that Denis the Areopagite, that most eager student of all things divine, wrote in his *Mystical Theology* that Blessed Bartholomew proved what a remarkable grasp of theology he had by stating that theology is at once the greatest and the least science. In fact, to understand that is to understand all things, and that is beyond the reach of any finite intellect. In his *The Names of God*, Denis says that God who is the Maximum, is neither this nor that, neither in one place nor in another, for being all things, He is not any one of them. And towards the end of his *Mystical Theology* he concludes: He is the one complete cause of all, unable to be limited in any form; He is so infinitely above all and independent of all that the suppression of all things would leave His pre-eminence unaffected. Hence he concludes, in his letter to Gaius, that God is known but that no mind or intelligence comprehends Him.

In accord with this is the statement of Rabbi Salomon that it is the unanimous opinion of wise men 'that the Creator is not apprehended by the sciences but He alone comprehends His own essence; by comparison, our apprehension has no means of approaching an understanding of Him'. Elsewhere, too, he writes: 'Praised be the Creator! To comprehend His nature the sciences are inadequate, wisdom is ignorance and pretentious language meaningless.' Therein lies that learned ignorance for which we are looking; by means of it alone, Denis strove in many ways to show that God could be found, starting from no other principle, I think, than the one I have mentioned.

The conclusion we reached from our consideration of the infinite straightness of the infinite curve may now be applied analogically to the most simple, infinite essence of the Maximum; how of all essences it is the one infinitely simple essence; how in it all the essences of things which have been or are still to be are always eternally in act its very essence; just as it is the essence of all, so is it all the essences; how it—the essence of all things—is each of them and none of them in particular, because it is all at once; and how, like the infinite line, which is the most adequate measure of all lines, the infinite essence is the most adequate measure of all essences.

For the Maximum—which is also the Minimum—is

necessarily the most exact measure of all things; it is not too great, since it is the Minimum, nor too small, because it is the Maximum. All that can be measured falls between the maximum and the minimum; therefore the infinite essence is the most adequate and precise measure of all essences.

To see this more clearly, think of two infinite lines, one consisting of an infinite number of feet, the other of lengths of two feet in infinite number; yet necessarily they would be equal, since infinity is not greater than infinity. As one foot is not smaller in an infinite line than two feet, so the matter of one or two feet in no way affects the length of the infinite line. Further, since each part of the infinite is infinite, then one foot of the infinite line is as equally the whole infinite line as two feet are.

Similarly, in the infinite essence every essence is the infinite essence itself; the Infinite is the sole, complete and precise measure of all essences. Apart from it no exact measure of any essence exists, for, as we have already most clearly proved, all others are defective and never as precise as they might be.

CHAPTER XVII. PROFOUND TRUTHS FROM THE PRECEDING CONSIDERATION

WE WILL CONTINUE OUR REFLECTIONS ON THE same subject. A finite line is divisible, whereas an infinite line, in which the maximum is one with the minimum, has no parts and is in consequence indivisible. The finite line, however, cannot be divided into anything but a line, for, as we have already seen, in dividing an extended object, we never reach a minimum point which is the smallest that can exist. The essence, therefore, of the finite line is indivisible: a line a foot long is as much a line as a line of an arm's length. We have no alternative but to conclude that the essential explanation of the finite line is the infinite line. The simple Infinite is thus the explanation of all, which is another way of saying that it is the measure of all. Aristotle, therefore, in his Metaphysics rightly asserts that the First Being is the rule and measure of all beings, because He is the essential explanation of all.

Moreover, in consequence of its indivisibility, the infinite line (the essential explanation of the finite line) is immutable and eternal; and these attributes equally must belong to the Reason of all things—God, ever to be blessed. In the light of this we can appreciate what the famous Denis meant when he said that the essence of things is incorruptible, and what others meant by calling the reason of things eternal; and in the Phaedo, the divine Plato—according to Chalcidius—has also maintained that there is but one model or idea of all things, and it really exists in itself; yet with regard to things which are multiple, there seem to be many models. When, in fact, I consider a two-feet line, a three-feet line and so on, I distinguish two things, namely, the essence of the line, which in each and every one of them is one and the same, and the difference which exists between the two-feet line, the three-feet line; and this makes it seem that the essence of the line of two feet is really distinct from the essence of the line of three feet. Now the essential explanation of the finite line is the infinite line and there is no doubt that in the infinite line there is no difference between the two-feet line and the three-feet line. In consequence, there is only one essence of the two lines and the diversity of things or of lines is not essential (for there is only one essence) but accidental, arising from the fact that they do not equally share the essence. Therefore, there is but one essence of all things, which in a diversity of ways is shared.

We proved earlier on that there cannot exist two things perfectly alike, or, in other words, it is impossible for two things to share the one essence in precisely the same way; it can only be in diverse manners that beings share the one essence. The power to share an essence with the most perfect equality is solely possessed by the Maximum or the Infinite Essence itself. Just as there is but one most perfect unity, so there can be only one equality of unity; and because this is the most perfect equality, it is the essence of all things.

Likewise, there is but one infinite line and it is the essence of all finite lines; and since the finite necessarily comes from the infinite line, by that very fact it can no more be its own essence than it can be at once finite and infinite. Consequently, just as it is impossible to have two precisely equal finite lines (since exact equality, which is the greatest equality, is Infinity itself), so it is also impossible to find two lines sharing equally the essence which is the one essence of all.

Moreover, as we have already said, in a line of two feet the infinite line is neither more nor less than two feet, in a line of three feet, neither more nor less than three feet and so on; it is entire in each finite line since it is one and indivisible. Yet it is not as finite and participated that it is entire in each; for if it were it could not be entire in a line of three feet while it was entire in one of two feet, because a two-feet line is not a three-feet line. It is, therefore, whole and entire in each, because it is none of them, and the distinction of one line from others is due to the fact that they are finite.

The infinite line, then, is entire in each line and each is in it. If we consider these two statements together—and we must— we clearly see how the Maximum is in each thing and in no one thing in particular. Since it is by the same essence that it is in each thing and each thing in it, and since it is itself this very essence, then it is no other than the Maximum, which is then the Maximum in se: The Maximum which is the rule and measure of all things is really one and the same as the Absolute Maximum in se: the Maximum is the Maximum. The Maximum alone of all beings exists in se, and all things are in it as in their own essence, because the Maximum is their essence.

These considerations, and in particular the simile of the infinite line, can be a great aid to the intellect as it moves forward in sacred ignorance towards the Absolute Maximum which is above all understanding. For since beings have only a participation in being, we now clearly see how we arrive at God by eliminating that participation from all beings; once that is suppressed there remains only entity in its infinite simplicity, which is the essence of all beings. It is only by the most learned ignorance that the mind grasps such an entity, for nothing seems to be left once I mentally remove all that has participated being. For that very reason Denis the Great says that an understanding of God is not so much an approach towards something as towards nothing; and sacred ignorance teaches me that what seems nothing to the intellect is the incomprehensible Maximum.

CHAPTER XVIII. FROM THE SAME CONSIDERATION WE LEARN THE MEANING OF THE PARTICIPATION OF BEING

THE IMMENSE INTELLECTUAL SATISFACTION GIVEN by the previous considerations serves merely as an incentive to our ever-inquisitive mind to go on and discover the way to a still clearer conception of this participation of the one Maximum; and in this it will again derive help from the example of the infinite straight line.

We learn from that example that a curve that is capable of being more curved or less curved cannot be the maximum or the minimum; and that a curve is not something, as curve, for it is a falling away from straightness. The maximum curve, as the minimum curve, is necessarily a straight line and consequently the entity of a curve is a participation of straightness. The less curved, then, a curve is (e.g. the circumference of a larger circle), the more it participates straightness, not in the sense that it takes a part (more) of it, for the infinite straight line is not divisible into parts; but the longer a finite straight line is, so much the more does it seem to participate the infinity of the absolute infinite line. The finite straight line, by reason of its straightness, enjoys a more direct and immediate participation of the infinite, whereas the curve's participation is rather remote and mediate: the minimum curve is reduced to straightness and it is then through straightness that it has participation. In like manner there are beings that participate more immediately in the infinite self-subsisting entity, e.g. simple finite substances, and there are others, e.g. accidents, whose participation is not direct but through their substances. Despite then the diverse forms of participation, straightness, as Aristotle says, is its own measure and that of the oblique; and just as the infinite line is the measure of the straight line and the curve, so the Maximum is the measure of all that in any way whatsoever participates being.

This makes clear the sense of the axiom: more or less does not change the nature of a substance. That is as true as this other statement: a finite straight line, in-so-far as it is straight, cannot be more or less straight; though by reason of their being finite and by their diverse forms of participation in the infinite, one line is more or less straight than another; two are never found that are equally straight. A curve, on the other hand, is susceptible of degrees as regards its participation of straightness; as with the straight line, so with the curve, the degrees of more and less are due to the different participations of straightness. That is why the grade of accidents is higher the greater its participation in the substance, and why it is higher still when its substance is of a higher order. From this it is clear how beings fall into one or other of two categories: either they participate the entity of the first (being) per se or through the intermediation of others, just as all lines are either straight or curved. Aristotle, on that account, classified all the beings of the world under substance and accidents.

Therefore, the one perfectly adequate measure of substance and accidents is the Absolute Maximum. Though not Himself substance or accidents, as we have already seen, yet by preference to accidents He is called Substance, as substances immediately participate His entity. Accordingly, of the two names 'Supersubstantial' and 'Superaccidental', Denis the Great chooses the former for the Maximum as more fitting by reason of its greater signification. The word 'supersubstantial' is used (here) to signify non-substantial, for, though supersubstantial signifies something or someone above substance, it does not adequately express the Maximum. It is, therefore, in a negative that we find a truer title for Him, as we shall see when we come to deal with the Names of God.

From the foregoing one could make a long study of the distinction and species of substances and accidents but there is no place for it here.

CHAPTER XIX. ANALOGY BETWEEN THE INFINITE TRIANGLE AND THE INFINITE TRINITY

WE CAN NOW LEARN OUR LESSON IN IGNORANCE from the thesis we established, viz. that the infinite line is an infinite triangle. We proved that the infinite line is a triangle; and since the line is infinite, the triangle will be infinite. Every angle of the triangle is a line, since the whole triangle is a line. Therefore, the infinite line is threefold. But there cannot be more than one infinite; therefore, that trinity is a unity.

Further, we know from geometry that the angle opposite the greater side is greater; but since the triangle here has only an infinite side, the angles will be the greatest possible, will be infinite. Consequently one is not smaller than the others nor are two greater than the third; in fact, it is as impossible for other angles to exist outside the one infinite angle, as it is for any quantity to exist outside infinite quantity. Therefore, one will be in another and all three will be the one infinite angle.

Moreover, as the infinite line is no more a line than a triangle, circle or sphere, but is in truth, as we saw, all of them without distinction, so we may equally consider the Absolute Maximum as the infinite line and call it essence, as the infinite triangle and call it trinity, as the infinite circle and call it unity, and as the infinite sphere and call it actual existence.

The Maximum is, therefore, a threefold essence which is actually one: the essence is not distinct from the trinity, nor the trinity from the unity, nor the actual existence from the unity, trinity or essence; yet without forming any sort of composition, essence, trinity, unity and actual existence are in the truest sense, one with the Maximum. These two truths, that the Maximum exists and is one, and the Maximum is a trinity, involve no contradiction between the trinity and the infinitely simple unity; the trinity is unity itself.

The only possible way of reaching this truth is by using the example of the infinite triangle. From our previous considerations we know, in-so-far as it is humanly possible, the true triangle and the infinite line; from this knowledge then, we shall, in learned ignorance, acquire a knowledge of the Trinity. For we see how the infinite triangle differs from the finite triangles: in finite triangles we find one angle, then another and finally a third; and because these angles are really distinct from one another, they can only form in the unity of triangle a unity of composition; whereas in the infinite triangle we find one angle which is three without being numerically multiplied. The most learned Augustine, on that account, justly remarks: 'From the moment you begin to count the Trinity, you depart from the truth.' In theology we must, as far as possible, forestall contradictories by previously uniting them in a simple concept; e.g. instead of regarding distinction and non-distinction as contradictories in theology, we must previously consider them in their infinitely simple principle in which there is no difference between distinction and non-distinction. We will then have a clearer idea of how trinity and unity are one and the same. Where, in fact, distinction is non-distinction, unity is trinity. This is equally applicable to the plurality of persons and the unity of essence, for where plurality is unity, the trinity of persons is the same as unity of essence; conversely, where unity is plurality, unity of essence is trinity in the persons.

All this is made evident by our example, in which the infinitely simple line is a triangle and conversely the infinite triangle is one line. It is also clear from this that the angles of this triangle cannot be numbered 1, 2 and 3, since they are all identified with one another: 'The Father is in Me and I in the Father,' as the Son says. In addition a true triangle must have three angles; most certainly, then, there are three angles here, and each is infinite and all are the one infinite. Moreover, the nature of a triangle demands that the angles should be distinct; here the nature of the infinite oneness of essence demands that these three angles be not really distinct but one angle. This also is verified here.

If, as I have suggested, you begin by previously uniting the apparent contradictories, you will not have 1 and 3 or 3 and 1 but a 'unitrinity' or 'triunity'. That is infinite truth.

CHAPTER XX. TEACHING ON THE TRINITY CONTINUED: IMPOSSIBIL- ITY OF HAVING FOUR OR MORE DIVINE PERSONS

FURTHER, BY ITS NATURE THE TRINITY, WHICH IS and is called a 'triunity', demands that the three be one. Now it is only from correlation and order that we can form any idea of this: correlation unites things that are distinct and order distinguishes them; e.g. in drawing a triangle we have first one angle, then another and finally from these two a third and these angles are so correlated that from them one triangle is formed; and in the infinite this is infinitely true. We must, however, take care to see that our concepts of priority and posteriority in eternity are not mutually exclusive; otherwise there could be no question of priority and posteriority in the Infinite and Eternal. The Father, in consequence, is not prior to the Son and the Son posterior to Him: the Father is prior in such a way that the Son is not posterior. The Father is First Person without the Son being second in time; just as the Father is First without priority, so the Son and the Holy Ghost are Second and Third respectively without being posterior. We need not dwell longer on this, as it has already received full enough treatment.

On the subject of the ever-blessed Trinity there is a point that is well worth noting, viz. that the Maximum is a trinity and that anything beyond a trinity in the maximum, e.g. 4, 5 or more would be in contradiction with its simplicity and perfection. The simplest figure to which any polygon can be reduced is the triangle, which is, in fact, the smallest polygon that can exist. But we have already proved that the absolute minimum coincides with the maximum. Therefore

44

what unity is in numbers, the triangle is in polygons, and just as every number is reduced to unity, so polygons are reduced to the triangle. The Maximum triangle, therefore, with which the minimum coincides, comprises all polygons, for the infinite triangle is to all polygons as infinite unity is to all numbers.

A four-sided figure is not the smallest figure; the triangle is evidently smaller than it. Because it is greater than the minimum, the four-sided figure is necessarily a composite; therefore it can find no place in the infinitely simple Maximum, which coincides with the minimum alone. In addition, Maximum and 'quadrangular' are mutually exclusive, for a four-sided figure is always greater than a triangle and could not therefore be the adequate measure of triangles. How could the Maximum be that which is not the measure of all? Besides, the quadrangle owes its existence to another, is a composite and is, in consequence, finite; how could such a being be the Maximum?

It is now evident, therefore, that potentially the simple line is, first of all, the simple triangle (as far as polygons are concerned), then the simple circle, then the simple sphere; and these elementary figures, which are the only ones educible from the potency of the simple line, cannot be reduced to one another in the finite, and between them they comprise all figures. It is, then, as if we wanted to form an idea of the measures of all measurable quantities; firstly, for the measure of length it would be necessary to have the maximum, infinite line, with which the minimum coincides; then, for rectilinear surface we should likewise require the infinite triangle, and for circular surface the infinite circle, and for depth the infinite sphere. With these four alone can all things measurable be measured. All these, of course, necessarily would be infinite and maximum measures with which the minimum would coincide; but since there cannot be more than one Maximum, we say that this unique Maximum, which is necessarily the measure of all quantities, is those measures without which it could not be the maximum measure. Yet when it is considered in itself, without reference to things measurable, it is not, nor can it truly be said to be any one of these: it is incomparably and infinitely above them. It is then because the simple Maximum is the measure of all things that we give it those names, which alone enable us to understand how it can be the measure of all. Thus we call the maximum a trinity, though it is infinitely above every trinity; but our reason for doing so is that we should be unable otherwise to understand that the maximum is the absolute cause, rule and measure of things whose oneness of essence is threefold; in figures, e.g. the unity of the triangle is the trinity of angles. Apart from that, however, both the word trinity and our idea of it fall infinitely short of the infinite and incomprehensible truth and in reality are not at all applicable to the Maximum.

Consequently we consider the infinite triangle as the infinitely simple measure of all things whose existence is threefold, like operations which are actions with a threefold existence, viz. in faculty, object and act; as also contrasts, beauty, relations, correlations, natural appetites and all other things whose unity of essence lies in a plurality; and particularly the being and operation of nature, which consists in the correlation of agent, patient and the effect produced by them.

CHAPTER XXI. ANALOGY BETWEEN THE INFINITE CIRCLE AND UNITY

HAVING COMPLETED OUR BRIEF TREATMENT OF the infinite triangle we will now go on to deal in a similar way with the infinite circle.

The circle is a perfect figure of unity and simplicity. We

have previously seen that the triangle is a circle; the trinity then is unity, and that unity is infinite as the circle is infinite; it is, therefore, infinitely more one or more identified with itself than any unity that is able to be represented by symbols and can be apprehended by us. In fact, this identity is so complete that it precedes even all relative distinctions, for in it distinction and diversity and identity are all one. Because of this infinite unity, all the attributes of the Maximum are the Maximum without diversity or distinction: in Him goodness is not one thing and wisdom another, they are one. In Him all diversity is identity: His power is so infinitely one that it is at once infinite and infinitesimal; and His duration is so infinitely one that past, present and future are there without any distinction, forming a duration that is most perfectly one without beginning or end, which is eternity.

In Him, in fact, the beginning is such that the end and the beginning are one.

All this we gather from the infinite circle, which having neither beginning nor end is eternal, is infinitely one and infinite in capacity. Now, because this circle is infinite, its diameter also is infinite; and the diameter is the circumference for this circle is infinitely one and there cannot be more than one infinite. But the middle of an infinite diameter is infinite, and, as the middle is the centre, it is evident that the centre, diameter and circumference are one and the same. The lesson we here learn in our ignorance is that the Maximum, which is at once the minimum, is incomprehensible; and in it the centre is the circumference.

You see how the Maximum in its simplicity and indivisibility is wholly and completely in the midst of all, because it is the infinite centre; how while outside all it encompasses all, because it is the infinite circumference; how it penetrates all because it is the infinite diameter. It is the beginning of all because it is the centre, the end of all because it is the circumference, the middle of all because it is the diameter. Because it is the centre it is the efficient cause, because it is diameter it is the formal cause, because it is the circumference it is the final cause. It gives being because it is the centre, it governs because it is diameter, it conserves in being because it is the circumference. And many similar conclusions could be drawn.

You understand, in consequence, how the Maximum is a being which is neither the same as, nor different from any other, and how all things are in it, from it and by it, because it is the circumference, diameter and centre. In reality it is not a circle, circumference, diameter or centre, but by reason of its infinite simplicity we have to study it by means of these comparisons and we discover that it encompasses all that exists and all that does not exist; so non-being in it is infinite being just as the minimum in it is the Maximum. It is the measure of all circular movements: from potency to act and back from act to potency; of all composition: from Primary elements to individuals and the resolution of individuals to their Primary elements; of perfect circular forms, circular operations and movements which turn on themselves and return to their beginnings; and similarly of all such movements whose unity consists in a perpetual cycle.

From this consideration of the circle many points about the perfection of unity could be deduced; but I omit them for the sake of brevity, as they are conclusions that each can discover with ease from the premisses. I would ask you especially to note how all theology is circular and lies within a circle, to such an extent even that the terms of the attributes are truly convertible: infinite justice is infinite truth, and infinite truth is infinite justice, and so it is with all of them. This enquiry, if you liked to continue it, could throw much light on an infinite number of points in theology up till now obscure.

CHAPTER XXII. IN THE PROVIDENCE OF GOD CONTRADICTORIES ARE RECONCILED

THAT WE MAY BE THE MORE CONSCIOUS OF THE deep insight we now have from our previous reflections, let us now turn to the study of God's Providence. It is clear, from what has been said, that God encompasses all things, even contradictories; it follows then that nothing escapes His Providence. Whether we have done this or its opposite or nothing at all—all was implicitly contained in God's Providence. Nothing will happen but in accordance with His Providence.

God, then, could have foreseen much that He has not foreseen nor will foresee; He has also foreseen much that He was able not to foresee; yet nothing can be added to divine Providence, nothing taken from it. To make a comparison: human nature is one and simple; were a man to be born who was never expected to be born, nothing would be added to human nature; if he had not been born, nothing would be taken from it, just as nothing is taken from it when those who have been born die. The explanation is that human nature embraces both those who are and those who neither are nor will be, though they could have been. Consequently, if even what never shall be should come to pass, nothing would be added to divine Providence, for it equally comprises actual events and those which, though possible, do not take place. Many of the potentialities of matter for ever remain in matter as mere possibilities and are never actualized; but, if all the things that are merely possible but never happen are objects of God's knowledge, His knowledge of them is not merely possible but actual knowledge, though from that it does not follow that these objects actually exist. Human nature, therefore, is said to comprise, and be comprised of, an infinite number of subjects, viz. not only men who have been, are and shall be, but those also who can be but never shall actually exist; thus human nature, while remaining unchanged, encompasses that variable content, just as infinite unity contains every number. So, too, is it with God's infinite Providence: it embraces what shall happen and what, though possible, shall not happen; and, in much the same way as a genus contains different species, it includes things contrary to one another. God's knowledge of things is not subject to the sequence of time, for He does not know the future as future nor the past as past, but He knows that all things are subject to change in His unchangeable eternity.

His Providence, then, is unchangeable, inevitable and all-embracing; therefore with reference to His Providence all things are rightly said to happen necessarily. All things, in fact, in God are God, and He Himself is absolute necessity. It is evident in consequence that those things which never shall happen are objects of God's foreknowledge in the way we have described, though they have been foreseen merely as possibilities. What God has foreseen He necessarily has foreseen, for His Providence is necessary and unchangeable; yet He was also able to foresee the opposite. To say that God's Providence is all-embracing does not mean that all within it has actual existence; on the other hand to say that a thing actually exists means that it is included in the scope of God's Providence. Though tomorrow, e.g. I can choose between reading and not reading, my choice, whichever it be, is known to Providence, for contraries are among its objects. Therefore, whatever I shall have chosen to do will be done in accordance with divine Providence.

It is clear then how we arrive at the truth on the Providence of God and similar subjects from the foregoing considerations, which show us the Maximum as a Being, to whom nothing stands in opposition, because all beings, in whatsoever way they be, are in Him and He in them.

CHAPTER XXIII. ANALOGY OF THE INFINITE SPHERE AND THE ACTUAL EXISTENCE OF GOD

I T WILL BE IN PLACE TO MAKE A FEW REFLECTIONS now on the infinite sphere. In it we discover three infinite lines of length, breadth and thickness meeting in the centre. But, because the centre of the infinite sphere is equal to the diameter and circumference, it is equal to those three lines; more than that, it is identified with all of them, with length, breadth and thickness. Consequently, the centre will be the absolutely simple and infinite Maximum and all length, breadth and thickness found in it are the absolutely simple and indivisible Maximum. Thickness is also the same thing as the circumference for the centre precedes all length, breadth and thickness and is the end and middle of all these, since it is the centre in the infinite sphere. Just as the infinite sphere is absolutely simple and wholly in act, so the Maximum is absolutely simple and wholly in act; and, just as the sphere is the act of the line, triangle and circle, so the Maximum is the act of all things. That explains why everything that has actual existence has its actuality from the Maximum, and how the degree of actual existence of every being is measured by its actuality in the Infinite itself. The Maximum, in consequence, is the form of forms and the form of being or the actual infinite entity.

This thought led to the very subtle reflection of Parmenides: 'God is the Being in Whom being anything means being everything.' As, therefore, the sphere is the absolutely ultimate perfection of figures, so the Maximum is the absolute perfection of all beings. That is so true that an imperfection in the Maximum is infinite perfection, just as the infinite line is a sphere, a curve is a straight line, composition is simplicity, diversity is identity, distinction is unity, and so on. How could there be any imperfection where imperfection is infinite perfection and possibility infinite act and so on?

Since the Maximum is, as it were, the infinite sphere, it is now evident how it is the unique, most simple and most adequate measure of the universe and all existing in it, because in the Maximum the whole is not greater than the part, just as the sphere is not greater than the infinite line. God, therefore, is the one infinitely simple, essential explanation of the entire universe. The sphere is generated after infinite revolutions, and God, as the infinite sphere, is the infinitely simple measure of all revolution. In fact, all life, movement and intelligence are from Him, in Him and through Him; and with Him a revolution of the 8th sphere is not smaller than one of the infinite sphere, because He is the end of all movement and in Him all movement finally comes to rest; for He is infinite repose in which all movement is rest. Just as infinite straightness is the measure of all circumferences and the infinite present or eternity the measure of all time, so infinite repose is the measure of all movements. In God, therefore, all movements come to rest as in their term, and every potentiality in Him, as in Infinite Act, is actualized. Because all movement is a tendency towards being, it must have its final term and so come to rest in Him who is the entity or form and act of all being.

He, therefore, is the final cause of all. But since beings are finite their attraction to Him as their end necessarily differs from one to another. Some are attracted through the intermediary of others, in much the same way as the line is to the sphere through the triangle and circle, the triangle to the sphere through the circle, and the circle directly to the sphere.

CHAPTER XXIV. NAME OF GOD AND POSITIVE THEOLOGY

WE HAVE BEEN ENDEAVOURING WITH GOD'S help to acquire a fuller knowledge in our ignorance of the Absolute Maximum by the aid of mathematical illustrations. To complete our knowledge let us now turn to the question of the Maximum. This enquiry should not entail much difficulty, if we have kept well in mind what has already been said often enough.

Since the Maximum is the Absolute infinite and therefore all things without distinction, it is clear that it cannot have a proper name. It is, in fact, the individual essence of a thing that makes it distinct from other things; it is from its individual essence that a thing is given its name. Where there is absolutely no distinction, then there can be no proper name.

Hermes Trismegistus for that reason rightly remarks: 'Because God is all things He has no proper name, for it would be necessary either to give Him every name or call all things by His name', since in His simplicity He is entirely all things. The name, Deus, which to us is a word of four letters (tetragrammaton) and unspeakable, is proper to Him, because it belongs to Him in virtue of His own essence and not through any reference to creatures; but it is a proper name that must be understood, according to Hermes, in the sense of 'One and All' or, better, 'All in One'. In an earlier chapter we learned of Infinite Unity, which is the same thing as 'All in One'; in fact, 'Unity' even still seems a better and more appropriate title than 'All in One'. It is for that reason that the Prophet says: 'God will be one in that day and His name one'; and in another place: 'Hear ye Israel (i.e. intellectual vision of God), for thy God is one.'

It is not in the sense in which we use the word unity nor in the way in which we understand it, that God is called unity. Being above all understanding, He is a fortiori above every name. It is reason (which is much lower than intellect) that gives names to things in order to distinguish them from one another. The reconciliation of contradictories is beyond reason, so to every name reason naturally opposes another; e.g. reason naturally opposes plurality or multitude to unity. God is not called 'Unity' in this sense, but 'Unity' in which distinction, plurality or multitude are all identified. For us it is the maximum name comprising as it does all things in its absolute unity; 'Deus' is a name that is ineffable and above our understanding.

Who can understand the infinite unity that infinitely transcends and precedes all distinction—which, without being a composite, embraces all in its absolute unity—in which there is neither diversity nor difference and where man does not differ from lion nor heaven from earth? Yet most truly they are there, not with their individual limitations but 'all in one', the Maximum unity itself. If, therefore, we could understand or find a name for such a unity, which, though one, is all things and which is at once the minimum and the maximum, we would have found the name of God. But since the title of God is God, His name is known only by that intellect which is itself the Maximum and is named the Maximum. Here, then, our learned ignorance teaches us that, though 'unity' seems the more appropriate title for the Maximum, yet it falls infinitely short of the Maximum's true name, which is *The* Maximum.

It clearly results from this that the names we affirm of God are given Him on account of a particular meaning they have when applied to creatures, and for that reason they can only apply to Him as diminutives that fall infinitely short of His real name. Since a term that is particular, that marks a distinction and that suggests its opposite, can only apply to God in the way we have described, affirmations, as Denis says, are unsuitable. If, for example, we call Him Truth, its opposite, falsity, comes to mind; if we call Him Virtue, vice is suggested; if we call Him Substance, we are confronted with accidents; and so it is with the others. He is a Substance, but a substance which is all things and to which nothing stands in opposition; He is the Truth, but truth which is all things without any distinction; these particular names, in consequence, can only be applied to Him as infinitely weak diminutives. Every affirmation puts, so to speak, in God something of the thing it signifies: but He is as much all things as He is something; therefore, all affirmations are inappropriate. If, therefore, affirmative names are used, they can only apply to Him in relation to creatures; and that does not mean that He is indebted to creatures for such names (the Maximum can receive nothing from creatures), but that they are His in virtue of His infinite power over creatures. Before time began God could have created, for otherwise He would not have been all-powerful; so the name, Creator, which may be applied to Him with reference to creatures, was also applicable before any creature existed, as it was in His power to create from eternity. The same holds good for justice and all the other affirmative names which we borrow from creatures and analogically give to God on account of the perfection these names express. But even before we attribute these names to Him, they were from eternity really included in His absolute perfection and infinite name, in the same way as were the things which such names stand for and from which we transferred them to God.

This is so true of all affirmations that even the names of the Trinity and of the Persons, Father, Son and Holy Spirit are bestowed in reference to creatures. For instance, because God is Unity, He is the Father who engenders; because He is the equality of unity, He is the Son who is engendered; because He is the connection of both these, He is the Holy Spirit; evidently, then, He is called the Son because He is the equality of unity either of entity or being. This makes it clear that the name Son is given Him in reference to those things also which God from eternity could have made, but did not create. For He is the Son because He is the equality of being—an equality that renders it impossible for more to exist or less to exist than this equality demands; in other words, He is the Son, because He is the equal even of the entity of the things which God was not going to create, though it was in His power to give them existence. To deny Him that power would be equivalent to saying that He is not the Father or the Son or the Holy Spirit; in fact, it would be a denial of God's existence. On closer scrutiny, therefore, you will see that the Father's begetting the Son meant the creation of all things in the Word. Accordingly we find Augustine calling the Word also the design and the ideal in relation to creatures. God, therefore, is Father because He engendered the equality of unity, He is the Holy Spirit because He is their mutual love. That all these terms are used in relation to creatures is evident from the fact that the beginning of a creature is due to God's being Father, its completion to God's being Son and its fitting in with the order of the universe to God's being the Holy Spirit. These traces of the Trinity are to be found in all things. This opinion is also expressed by Aurelius Augustine in his commentary on the words of Genesis: 'In the beginning God created heaven and earth', where he says that it was as Father that God created things in their beginnings.

All affirmations, therefore, that are made of God in theology are anthropomorphic, including even those most holy Names, which enshrine the highest mysteries of divine knowledge and were used by the Hebrews and the Chaldeans. Each of them expresses only a particular attribute of God; and there is no proper name of God save that four-lettered word, ioth —he—vau—he, which in our earlier explanation we called unspeakable. Jerome and Rabbi Salomon in the book *Dux Neutrorum* deal at length with these and can be consulted.

CHAPTER XXV. VARIOUS ANTHROPOMORPHISMS USED BY PAGANS

IN A SIMILAR WAY PAGANS TOOK THEIR NAMES FOR God from the different qualities of creatures. They called him Jupiter, for example, because of his remarkable goodness (Jupiter, according to Julius Firmicus, is so favourable a planet that, if he alone had sway in heaven, men would be immortal). They named him also Saturn on account of the sublimity of his ideas and his ingenuity in regard to the necessities of life; Mars because of victories in war; Mercury on account of his counsels; Venus because of the love that preserves nature; the Sun because he is the power behind the physical changes in the universe; the Moon because of the conservation of the life-giving humours; Cupid on account of the mutual love of the two sexes. He was also called Nature for the same reason, as it is by the duality of the sexes that he preserves the different species of things. Among all beings— animals and non-animals—Hermes maintained that two sexes are found; and he argued, in consequence, that the Cause of All, God, comprised in Himself the masculine and feminine sexes, of which he believed Venus and Cupid were a manifestation. Valerius Romanus also shared this view and sang of an omnipotent Jupiter who was God the father and God the mother. Their conclusion was that Cupid (so-called from one thing's desiring another) was the daughter of Venus, the goddess of natural beauty, and that Venus herself was the daughter of Jupiter, the omnipotent author of Nature and all that attends on Nature.

Their temples and similar monuments are further evidence that the Pagans ascribed to God the names of various perfections found in creatures; e.g. we have the Temples of Peace, Eternity, Concord and the Pantheon; and in the middle of the Pantheon in the open air an altar was erected to the Infinite Term which is without term. All these names express what the one ineffable Name implies; and since the proper Name is Infinite it includes all the numberless names that denote particular perfections. Numerous as such names may be they are never so many or so great that they could not be added to, for each of them is to the proper and ineffable Name what the finite is to the infinite. The pagans of old ridiculed the Jews for adoring a God unique and infinite whom they did not know, whilst they themselves were adoring Him in his manifestations, adoring Him, in other words, wherever they beheld His divine works. Men at that time were unanimous in admitting the existence of the one infinite God than whom no greater could exist; they differed in-so-far as some, like the Jews and Sissennii, adored Him in His infinitely simple unity which comprised all things, whilst others, who saw in a sensible sign a guide to its cause and principle, worshipped Him wherever they found a manifestation of the Deity.

The simple folk were led into error by this latter method, for instead of regarding those sensible expressions as an image they took them for the truth itself. The result of this was that the masses became idolaters, whereas philosophers, for the most part, continued to have a correct idea of the unity of God, as can be attested to by anyone who has carefully read the ancient philosophers and Cicero's *De Deorum Natura*.

We do not deny that some pagans did not understand how

God, who is the entity of things, could exist outside things, in any other way than by a process of abstraction,—just as the existence of primary matter apart from things is due solely to intellectual abstraction. Such as these adored God in creatures and bolstered up their idolatry with arguments from reason. Some thought that God could be called on in prayer: the Sissennii, e.g. invoked him in the angels, the Gentiles in trees, such as the Sun tree and the Moon tree; others in the air, water or with a set form of prayers in temples. Our previous considerations show how misled they were and how far they wandered from the truth.

CHAPTER XXVI. NEGATIVE THEO-LOGY

THE WORSHIP OF GOD, WHO IS TO BE ADORED IN spirit and truth, necessarily rests on dogmatic assertions about Him; for that reason the cult in every religion is necessarily developed by affirmative theology: God is adored as one and three, as The Most Wise, The Most Good, The Light Inaccessible, The Life, The Truth and so on; and worship always is regulated by a faith which is acquired more surely through learned ignorance. By faith, for example, it is acknowledged that He who is adored as one is one and all; that He who is worshipped as Light Inaccessible, is not light that is material, the opposite of which is darkness, but light absolutely simple and infinite in which darkness is infinite light; that He who is infinite light itself shines always in the darkness of our ignorance, but the darkness cannot comprehend the Light. Negative Theology, in consequence, is so indispensable to affirmative theology that without it God would be adored, not as the Infinite but rather as a

creature, which is idolatry, or giving to an image what is due
to Truth alone. It will be useful, then, to add a few words on
negative theology.

Sacred ignorance has taught us that God is ineffable, because He is infinitely greater than anything that words can
express. So true is this that it is by the process of elimination
and the use of negative propositions that we come nearer the
truth about Him. For that reason the most noble Denis would
not have Him called Truth or Intellect or Light or any name
that man can utter; and in this he was followed by Rabbi
Salomon and all the wise. According to this negative theology,
therefore, He is neither Father nor Son nor Holy Ghost; one
word alone may be used of Him: Infinite. Infinity, as such,
does not engender, is not engendered and does not proceed,—
which called from Hilary of Poitiers, whilst distinguishing
the Persons, these subtle words: 'In aeterno infinitas, species in
imagine, usus in munere.' His meaning is that all we see in
eternity is infinity; and, while it is true that infinity is eternity,
yet infinity is a negative and for that reason it cannot be conceived as a principle of generation. Eternity, on the other hand,
clearly can be so conceived, for eternity is an affirmation of
infinite unity or of the infinite present, and is, therefore, a
principle that does not proceed from any other. 'Species in
imagine' expresses the principle that proceeds from a principle
and 'usus in munere' signifies procession from both.

All that is clear enough from what we have already said.
We know, in fact, that eternity is infinity, and that both of
these belong to the Father in the same way. Yet considered in
one way eternity is an attribute of the Father but not of the
Son nor of the Holy Ghost, whereas infinity belongs to all the
persons equally. Considered from the point of view of unity,
infinity is the Father, from the point of view of equality of
unity it is the Son, from the point of view of the connection
it is the Holy Ghost; but when considered, not from any of

these points of view, but absolutely in itself infinity says nothing of Father, Son and Holy Ghost, nor does it say anything of unity or plurality in God. And according to negative theology infinity is all we discover in God. Yet the fact is that infinity, as well as eternity, is each of the Three Persons and conversely each of the Persons is infinity and eternity. As far as negative theology is concerned, then, we must conclude that God cannot be known in this life or in the life to come. God alone knows Himself; He is as incomprehensible to creatures as infinite light is to darkness.

From this it is clear how in theology negative propositions are true and affirmative ones inadequate; and that of the negative ones those are truer which eliminate greater imperfections from the infinitely Perfect. It is truer, for example, to deny that God is a stone than to deny that He is life or intelligence,—truer to deny that He is intemperate than to deny that He is virtuous. In affirmative propositions the contrary holds good: it is truer to assert that God is intelligence and life than to assert that He is earth, stone or anything material.

All these points, which must now be abundantly clear, leave us with the conclusion that, in a way we cannot comprehend, absolute truth enlightens the darkness of our ignorance. That, then, is the learned ignorance for which we have been searching. We have shown how the sole approach to the Maximum—the Triune God of infinite Goodness—passes through the stages of that ignorance which is learning, and how, in consequence, amidst all our gropings, we can always praise Him, the Incomprehensible, for His revelation of Himself to us.

May He be blessed above all for ever.

THE SECOND BOOK

PROLOGUE

WE HAVE EXPOUNDED BY MEANS OF symbols what the science of ignorance has taught us about the nature of the Absolute Maximum. Using the same method and with the little light we have gained from the science of ignorance, let us now go on to study the Universe which totally depends on the Absolute Maximum for its existence.

Being an effect it has nothing from itself, but owes all to its cause, and stands in the closest resemblance possible to its cause and raison d'être. The difficulty, in consequence, of discussing the nature of the effect whilst its Absolute Model remains unknown, will escape no one. It was well, therefore, we took a course in the science of ignorance, not that it brought Absolute Truth within our grasp but it gave us a knowledge we could not have reached; and the consequence is that we are at least in a position to see that Absolute Truth exists, though we are still unable to comprehend it. To establish this is the purpose of this book. I leave you in your goodness to judge the worth of my effort.

CHAPTER I. FROM PROPOSITIONS ALREADY ESTABLISHED THE UNITY AND INFINITY OF THE UNIVERSE IS INFERRED

THE DOCTRINE OF IGNORANCE WILL BENEFIT considerably, if, by way of preface, we recall the inferences already drawn from our principle. Besides facilitating further deductions that can with like skill be made on a host of similar points, they will also throw light on what has to follow.

We have taken it as a fundamental principle that where degrees of difference are found it is impossible to arrive at a maximum which is actual and the greatest possible. From that we went on to see that absolute equality is predicable of God alone, with the result that, apart from Him, all beings necessarily differ from one another. No movement, therefore, can be the equal of another nor can one be the measure of another by reason of the necessary difference existing between the measure and the measured.

This should prove valuable to you in innumerable ways. If, for instance, you turn to astronomy you find its calculations lack precision because it has been taken for granted that the movement of all the other planets can be measured by the sun's movement. It is likewise impossible to have precise knowledge of the plan of the heavens with regard to any sort of place or with regard to the rise and setting of the stars or the elevation of the pole and all that lies around it. Since the factors of time and space cannot be precisely the same in any two places, it is evident that precision in detail is by no means to be expected in the judgments of astronomers.

If, turning to geometry next, you apply this rule of mathematics, you see that no two figures nor any two magnitudes can be perfectly equal: actual equality is here impossible. Though the rules laid down for describing a figure equal to a given figure may be theoretically exact, yet between the different concrete figures there can be no perfect equality. From that you arrive at an exact idea of equality, which is equality stripped by the intellect of material qualities; and that is true equality, which no amount of experimental knowledge could give you, for only degrees of it are to be found in things.

In music also our rule is verified. It is impossible to find two things that are perfectly equal in weight, or length, or thickness; and it is likewise impossible for the various notes of flutes and other instruments, of bells and of the human voice to be so perfectly in concord that they could not be more concordant. As with human voices, so it is with instruments, all are only relatively true and all differ necessarily according to place, time, natural characteristics and so on. Consequently the most perfect, faultless harmony cannot be perceived by the ear, for it exists not in things sensible but only as an ideal conceived by the mind. From this we can form some idea of the most perfect or infinite harmony, which is a relation in equality. No man can hear it while still in the body, for it is wholly spiritual and would draw to itself the essence of the soul, as infinite light would attract all light to itself. Such infinitely perfect harmony, in consequence, would be heard only in ecstasy by the ear of the intellect, once the soul was free from the things of sense. Much of the sweetness of contemplation could be experienced here by a meditation on the immortality of the intellectual and rational soul and on that essential incorruptibility, which enables it to find in music an image of itself that is at once a resemblance and a contrast; and this same sweetness could also be derived from a meditation on the eternal joy which is the lot of the blessed after the death of the body. We shall have something to say elsewhere of the eternal joy of the blessed.

Further, if we apply our rule to arithmetic, we see that where there are two there is necessarily a difference; and a numerical variation involves a variation to infinity of all things: composition, combination, proportion, harmony, change and so on,—a fact which explains to us why we are ignorant.

No two men are identical in anything; their sense perceptions differ, their imaginations differ, their intellects differ; and their activities, whether they take the form of writing, painting or any other form of art, are all different. Even if for a thousand years one man zealously tried to imitate another on some one point, he would never come to reproduce it exactly, though at times it may be that the difference is not perceived by the senses. Art, as far as possible, imitates nature, but it will never be able to reproduce it precisely as it is. We find, also, that medicine, alchemy, magic and the other arts of transmutation do not arrive at absolute truth, though, it need hardly be said, comparatively one is truer than another; medicine, for example, is truer than the arts of transmutation.

From this same principle we draw this conclusion: where there are opposites, like simple and composite, abstract and concrete, formal and material, corruptible and incorruptible, there we find degrees; hence a point is never reached where all opposition completely ceases or where the two are absolutely identical. All things are constituted of opposites in varying degrees; and having in them more of one and less of another, they take their nature from the dominant opposite. The purpose, then, of any rational enquiry is to find out how in one thing there is composition in simplicity and in another simplicity in composition, how in one corruptibility exists in incorruptibility and vice versa in another, and so on. With this point we shall deal more fully in our book *De Coniecturis*; but here these few remarks may suffice as evidence of the extraordinary efficacy of learned ignorance.

To keep more to our plan, I repeat that it is absolutely impossible to arrive either at a maximum or a minimum, for, from our study of number and the division of a continuum, we know well that we can never proceed to infinity. Since that is so, it clearly follows that, for any given finite being, a greater or lesser—in power, quantity, perfection, etc.—can always be found. To say that degrees of more and less are able to exist where, by supposition, the infinite is reached is a contradiction, for each part of the infinite is infinite. Degrees, therefore, cannot be admitted in the infinite; nor could they exist in that which would be in some way proportionate to the infinite, for it also would be infinite. Even if we were to grant the possibility of an actually infinite number, two in such a number would not be less than a hundred; nor would an infinite line made up of an infinite number of lines two feet long be smaller than an infinite line composed of an infinite number of lines of four feet. It is in God's power to give existence to all that is able to exist. Unless, therefore, God were to give the absolute maximum at once (which in the Third Book we shall see He did), then He is able to create more or less than He actually does create.

The Absolute Maximum alone is negatively infinite and for that reason it alone is all that it is able to be. The universe, on the other hand, cannot be negatively infinite, for, though it embraces all else, it does not include God; yet, if we consider it as termless and privatively infinite in consequence, we would have to say that it is neither finite nor infinite. It cannot, in fact, be greater than it is, for this reason that possibility or matter lacks the power to extend beyond itself. To say that 'the universe is always capable of being actually greater' is equivalent to saying that 'possible being passes to actual infinite being', which is absurd; for infinite actual being, which is absolute eternity, is the actualization of the entire possibility of being and that could not arise from possibility. Therefore, from the point of view of God's infinite or limitless power, the universe could be greater; but from the point of view of possibility or matter, which is incapable of actual, infinite extension, it cannot be greater. Since, then, nothing that would be a limit to the universe, by being greater than it, is able actually to exist, we may call the universe limitless and so privatively infinite. Its actual existence is limited by its nature so that its existence is the best that the condition of its nature permits. It is a creature and necessarily owes its existence to the Absolute Being, God. This with our science of ignorance we will go on to show briefly but as clearly and as simply as possible.

CHAPTER II. THE BEING OF A CREA-TURE COMES IN A MYSTERIOUS WAY FROM THE BEING OF THE MAXIMUM

FROM THE FOREGOING LESSONS IN SACRED IGNORANCE we have learned that God alone is 'a se', that in Him 'a se', 'in se', 'per se', and 'ad se' are all one, that He is, in other words, the Absolute; we learned, too, that necessarily every essence is indebted to Him for whatever existence it possesses. Otherwise, how could a being that is not 'a se' exist, if it did not receive its existence from the Eternal Being? As jealousy has no place in God, He cannot give a reduced form of being as such, so that the corruptibility, divisibility, imperfection, diversity, plurality, and other things of this kind, which are found in creatures that come from Him, are not attributable to Him, the Maximum, who is eternal, indivisible, most perfect,

simple, one; nor have such things any positive cause. We
have already shown that the infinite line is infinite straightness
and as infinite straightness it is the cause of all linear being; the
curve, on the other hand, qua line is from the infinite, qua curve
it is not; in fact, curvature is a consequence of finiteness: a curve
is a curve because it is not infinite; it would cease, in other
words, to be a curve if it were infinite. So also is it with things:
that they have being in a reduced form, that they are diverse and
distinct and have other similar marks of imperfection are not
effects of any cause; they are the consequences of their nature
which cannot be other than finite. Therefore, what is attributable to God is the fact that a creature has unity, separate existence and is in harmony with the universe; and the greater its
unity, the greater its resemblance to God; but it is an effect of
its contingent nature—not attributable to God or any positive
cause—that its unity is in a plurality, its individual existence
amidst confusion and its harmony amidst discordancy.

   Is it possible, then, for anyone to understand the being of a
creature by considering at once the absolute necessity which
produced it, and the contingency which is for it an indispensable condition of existence? A creature is not God, nor is it
nothing; it is, as it were, posterior to God and prior to nothing,
or it stands between God and nothing, according to one of the
sages: God is the opposite of nothing with being as the intermediary. And yet it cannot be a compound of being and non-
being. It seems, therefore, that it is neither being, for it is
derived from being, nor non-being, for it is prior to nothing,
nor a compound of these; and in considering these separately
or conjointly, our intellect, which is unable to reconcile contradictories, does not comprehend the being of a creature, though
it knows that every creature has its being from the Maximum.
As being ab alio, it is unintelligible, since the being from
whom it comes is incomprehensible—just as the being of an
accident is not intelligible, as long as its subject of inhesion is

not understood. The creature, qua creature, therefore, cannot be called one, since it is derived from unity; it cannot be said to be more than one, since it owes its being to unity; nor can it be at once one and more than one. In virtue of its nature its unity lies in a plurality. What we have said here ought equally to be applied, it seems, to simplicity and composition and the other contradictories.

Since the creature is created by the being of the Maximum, and since in the Maximum there is no difference between being, doing and creating, then it seems that it is one and the same thing to say that God creates as to say that God is all things. If, then, creation means that God is all things, how can the creature be conceived as other than eternal, when the being of God is eternal, or better, eternity itself? No one doubts its eternity in-so-far as the creature itself is the being of God; in-so-far, therefore, as it is temporal it is not from God, for He is eternal. How reconcile a creature's being at once temporal and eternal? Necessarily the creature's existence was possible from eternity in the Being; yet it was not possible for it to exist prior to time, for before time there was no 'before'; consequently it has always been when it was possible for it to be.

How is it possible, then, for anyone to understand how God is the form of being without being involved in creation? A composite can be formed only by beings between which there is some proportion; the infinite line and the finite curve, therefore, are unable to form a composite whole, for it is evident to all that between the infinite and the finite there is no possible proportion. How, then, can the intellect grasp that the curved line has its being from the infinite straight line, which, though not its informing form, is its cause and raison d'être? The curve cannot share the essence of the infinite line by taking part of it, since it is an infinite and indivisible essence; nor can it share it as matter shares the form, as Socrates and Plato, for example, share the human form; nor as parts share in the whole, as, for example, the universe shared by its parts; nor does it share it as several mirrors may be said to share in different ways the same face; for a mirror is a mirror before it receives the image of the face, whereas a creature is nothing if it is not 'ab esse': 'ab esse' is its very definition.

A creature is not a positively distinct reality that receives the image of the infinite form; it is merely the image and nothing more, and in different creatures we see accidentally different images of that form. Since that is so, how is it possible for us to understand that the various creatures share in different ways the one infinite form? It is as if a work of art were to have no other being than that of dependence, and of total dependence on the idea of the artist, from whom it would receive its being and by whose power it would be conserved in being; or it is like the image of the face in the mirror, provided we suppose that the mirror in itself and of itself is nothing before or after the reflection.

We are also unable to understand how God can manifest Himself to us through visible creation. He is not like our intellect, which is only known to Him and us; which, before coming to think, had no form, but proceeds, when thinking, to take the form of colour, sound, or something else from the images in the memory; then, after taking on another form of signs, words or letters, it manifests itself to others. God does not manifest Himself in that way. Whether His purpose in creating the world was to manifest His goodness, as pious people believe, or whether, as the Infinite Necessity, He created it to do His Will and have creatures who would be obliged to obey Him, who would fear Him and who would be judged by Him, it is clear whatever His purpose may have been, that He does not assume another form, since He is the form of all forms; and it is likewise clear that He does not manifest Himself in positive signs, for these signs, if they existed, would naturally in their turn demand others in which to exist, and so on to infinity.

Who can understand how all things, whilst different from one another by reason of their finite nature, are an image of that unique infinite form? God, so to speak, is incidentally brought to view in a creature, in the same way as a substance, so to speak, is incidentally presented to us by an accident and a man incidentally reproduced in a woman. Only in a finite fashion is the infinite form received. Every creature is, as it were, 'God-created' or 'finite-infinity', with the result that no creature's existence could be better than it is. It is as if the Creator had said 'Let it be produced', and, because God, who is eternity itself, could not be brought into being, that was made which could most resemble God. The inference from this is that every creature, as such, is perfect, though by comparison with others it may seem imperfect. God in His infinite goodness gives being to all in the way in which each can receive it. With Him there is no jealousy; He communicates being without distinction; and, since all receive being in accord with the demands of their contingent nature, every creature rests content in its own perfection, which God has freely bestowed upon it. None desires the greater perfection of any other; each loves by preference that perfection which God has given it and strives to develop and preserve it intact.

CHAPTER III. IN A MYSTERIOUS WAY THE MAXIMUM ENVELOPS AND DEVELOPS ALL THINGS

THE FIRST PART OF THIS WORK CONTAINS ALL THAT can be said or thought about truth in-so-far as it is subject to investigation. All that is in agreement with what we said there of the first truth is necessarily true; all that conflicts with it is false. There it was shown that, above all others, there must be one sole Maximum, which is at once all things and in which even the minimum and maximum are identified. As unity unites all, the Maximum, which is infinite unity, must envelop all; and it is not simply the maximum as unity, which comprises every number, but it is the Maximum because it envelops all things. Just as in number, which is a development of unity, only unity is to be found, so in all things which exist only the Maximum is to be found.

Quantity is a development of unity, and here unity is called a point, since there is nothing but a point to be found in quanity; just as there is nothing to be found in a line, no matter where you may divide it, but a point, so there is nothing in a surface or a solid but a point. There is one point, not more; and that one point is infinite unity itself, for infinite unity, whilst it contains within itself the line and quantity, is the point which is their term, perfection and entirety; and its first development is the line, in which there is nothing to be found but the point.

In the same way rest is unity, in which all movement is contained for on close examination movement is seen to be rest drawn out in an orderly series. Movement, therefore, is the first development of rest. In like manner all time is comprised in the present or 'now'. The past was present, the future shall be present, so that time is only a methodical arrangement of the present. The past and the future, in consequence, are the development of the present; the present comprises all present times, and present times are a regular and orderly development of it; only the present is to be found in them. The present, therefore, in which all times are included, is one: it is unity itself. So, too, is diversity contained in identity, inequality in equality, divisions or distinctions in simplicity. There is not an all-inclusive maximum of substances, another of quality or quantity, and so on; there is one sole Maximum which embraces all things,— the maximum, which is also the minimum, and in which the inclusion of diversity in identity is not a contradiction. Just as unity precedes distinction, so the point, which is perfection, precedes magnitude, for that which is perfect is prior to all that is imperfect: rest is prior to movement, identity to diversity, equality to inequality, and so on for all that is convertible with unity. Unity is convertible with eternity, for there cannot be more than one Eternal. God, therefore, envelops all in the sense that all is found in Him; He is the development of all in the sense that He is found in all.

To make this clear let us take an example. Number, which is a development of unity, presupposes an act of reason. Reason is a faculty of the soul, and it is because animals have no soul that they cannot count. Number, then, is accounted for by our mind, which distinguishes the many individuals that share a common nature; and similarly the plurality of things is accounted for by God's mind, in which by reason of its all-embracing unity, the multiplicity of things exists without plurality. Things cannot share in precisely the same way the equality of being. Plurality, which in Him is unity, has arisen from the fact that in His eternity He has understood one thing existing in one way, another in another way. It is unity that gives to plurality or number the only being it has. Without unity number would be impossible, for plurality can only be explained as a development of unity; unity, therefore, exists in plurality. How all is in one and one in all is above our understanding. Knowing, as we do, that God's understanding is His being and that His being is infinite unity, how could any of us understand that God's mind is the origin of the plurality of things?

If—continuing with our example of number—we consider that number is the mind's measurement of a multitude by a unit common to all, it would seem as though God, who is the unit, were multiplied in things, since His understanding is His being; and yet we know that any multiplication of that unit, which is the infinite maximum unity, is impossible. How, then, is plurality conceivable without a multiplication of the unit from which it has its being? or how are we to understand multiplicity in unity, if there is no multiplication? In one species, it may be said, there is a plurality of individuals and in one genus a plurality of species; but there is this difference that apart from the individuals the genus or species has no existence outside the abstracting intellect.

God's being, which is unity, is not abstracted by the mind from things, nor is it united to or immersed in things; it is, therefore, beyond anyone to understand how the plurality of things is a development of the unity which is God. If we consider things without Him, they are as number without unity: nothing; if we consider Him without things, He exists and the things do not; if we consider Him as He is in things, we are regarding things as something else in which He exists—an error which we pointed out in the last chapter, where we saw that the being of a thing is from the Being, God, and cannot, therefore, be 'other' in the sense of being totally different; if we consider a thing such as it is in God, then it is God and Unity.

All that remains for us to assert is that the plurality of things is due to the fact that God is in nothing. Take away God from the creature and you are left with nothing; take away the substance from a composite being, the accidents also disappear and nothing remains. Is it possible for the human mind to grasp this? The accident ceases to exist when the substance is removed, and its ceasing to exist in that instance is due to the fact that to inhere is of the nature of an accident and that its subsistence is the subsistence of the substance. Yet it cannot be said that an accident is nothing, for while it inheres in its substance it confers something on it; e.g. it is by quantity that a substance is quantified. This does not apply here, since the creature does not inhere in God in that manner. An accident gives something to a substance, the creature contributes nothing to God; in fact, an accident gives so much to a substance that, although the accident has its being from the substance, the substance cannot exist without any accident; but this can in no way apply to God.

The creature comes from God, yet it cannot, in consequence of that, add anything to Him who is the Maximum. How are we going to be able to form an idea of creature as such? If the creature as such is really nothing and has not even as much entity as an accident, how are we to accept as explanation of the development of the plurality of things the fact that God is in nothing, since nothing cannot be predicated of any entity? If you say: 'all theology is circular; God's will is the omnipotent cause, and He is His will and His omnipotence', you are thereby necessarily admitting that you are completely ignorant of how it comes about that God in His unity embraces all, whilst His unity is developed in plurality; you are simply admitting that you are conscious of your ignorance of the method even though you may know the fact that God's unity embraces all: all in God is God, all things come from His unity and in all things He is what they are, like truth in an image. It is as if a face were reproduced in its own image. With the multiplication of the image we get distant and close reproductions of the face. (I do not mean distance in space but a gradual distance from the true face, since without that multiplication would be impossible.) In the many different images of that face one face would appear in many, different ways, but it would be an appearance that the senses would be incapable of recognizing and the mind of understanding.

CHAPTER IV. HOW THE UNIVERSE, WHICH IS ONLY A RESTRICTED FORM OF MAXIMUM, IS A LIKENESS OF THE ABSOLUTE

IF WE ARE READY TO GO ON AND MAKE AN ADROIT USE of what learned ignorance has taught us in the previous chapters, in particular if we simply recall that all things are, or owe their existence to, the Absolute Maximum, we will be able to discover a good deal about the world or universe. For me the universe is only a restricted form of maximum. It is restricted or concrete, because it holds all its being from the Absolute; and because it is a maximum, it reproduces the Absolute Maximum in the greatest way possible. We may affirm, therefore, that all we learned in the First Book of the Absolute Maximum as belonging to Him without any restriction whatsoever, may be applied in a relative way to the restricted maximum.

Let us take some examples to help the student in his enquiry. God is the absolute Maximum and absolute unity, and, as such, He forestalls and unites things different and distant; e.g. contradictories, between which there is no mean, are identified in Him. In an absolute way He is what all things are; He is the absolute beginning in all, the end of all and the entity of all. Just as the infinite line is all the figures so the Absolute Maximum, in its infinite simplicity and unity, is all things without plurality. The world or universe is also a maximum though a limited maximum; it anticipates in its unity limited opposites like contraries; within its limited existence it is what all things are; and in a restricted sense it is the beginning, end and being of things. It is infinity contracted to the relatively infinite; and just as the relative maximum line is relatively all figures so the limited maximum—the universe—in its relative simplicity and unity is all things without plurality.

All becomes clear, then, once we have a correct idea of this contraction. In fact, the relative infinity or simplicity or unity in the universe comes from, though it is infinitely inferior to, the absolute, with the result that the infinity, eternity and unity of the world bear no comparison with the infinity, eternity and unity of the absolute. On that account absolute unity admits no plurality, whereas the unity of the universe does; for, though the universe is one and even a maximum from the point of view of unity, it is a relative unity and only a relative maximum. · Therefore, maximum unity though it be, its unity is limited by plurality, just as its infinity is by finiteness, its simplicity by composition, its eternity by succession and so on. It is as if absolute necessity were to communicate itself without fusion to another and find in that other a term that restricted it; or as if, independently of the intellect's act of abstraction, absolute whiteness were to exist in itself; any relatively white object would receive its whiteness from it and an object would be white only in-so-far as it received whiteness; in other words, in any object absolute whiteness would find itself limited by non-whiteness.

Much can be deduced from these considerations by the student. For instance, just as God, by reason of His Immensity, is neither in the sun nor the moon, yet in an absolute way he is in them what they are. So the universe is neither in the sun nor in the moon, yet in a restricted fashion it is in them what they are. No distinction can be made between the absolute quiddity of the sun and moon, for it is God Himself Who is the absolute entity and quiddity of all. But the restricted quiddity of the sun is distinct from the restricted quiddity of the moon, because the restricted quiddity of a thing is the thing itself, whereas the absolute quiddity is God and not the thing itself. For that reason it is evident that in the universe identity consists in diversity as unity consists in plurality, for the universe is a restricted quiddity, which in the sun is restricted in one way and in the moon in another. The universe, then, is not the sun nor the moon, yet it is the sun in the sun and the moon in the moon; on the other hand, God is not the sun in the sun nor the moon in the moon but He is without plurality and diversity what the sun and moon are. Universe means universality, i.e. unity of distinct things. Therefore the relationship of the universe to all things is that of humanity to men: humanity is neither Socrates nor Plato, but in Socrates it is Socrates and in Plato it is Plato.

Having established that the universe is only a principle and a maximum in a restricted sense, we can see now that the entire universe was brought into being by a simple emanation of the restricted maximum from the absolute maximum. The opinion of Avicenna and other philosophers that intelligences were created first, the spiritual soul next and then nature is not acceptable. All the beings which form parts of the universe must have come into being together with the universe, for without them it would be impossible for the universe in its limited nature to be one, entire and perfect. In the artist's mind the whole is conceived before the part, for example the house, before a wall; and so it was with the mind of God to Whose will all things owe their being. First, then, to be produced was the universe and, as a consequence, all that the existence of the universe and its perfection necessarily demanded. We consider the Absolute Maximum at first in the restricted maximum with a view to finding it afterwards in all the individuals, like the abstract in the concrete; for the Absolute Maximum exists in an absolute way in the universe. In fact, God is the absolute quiddity of the world or universe, whereas it is a restricted quiddity that forms the universe. Contraction means being restricted to some particular thing. The universe, therefore, in a restricted fashion, exists in all the particular beings that form it, whilst God, Who is one, is in the universe as a unity.

In this way we will be able to understand how God, Who is unity in its infinite simplicity, exists in the universe as a unity and, as a consequence, in all things through the intermediary of the universe; how, too, through the universe as a unity the plurality of things is in God.

CHAPTER V. EVERYTHING IN EVERY-THING

FROM A KEEN STUDY OF WHAT HAS ALREADY BEEN said we come to understand easily enough, perhaps even more fully than Anaxagoras himself, the depth of the truth he expressed in the words 'everything is everything'. For from the First Book we learned that God is in all things in such a way that all things are in him; in the previous chapter we discovered that God is in all things by the medium, as it were, of the universe; so it follows that all is in all, and each in each. As if by nature's order it was that the most perfect—the universe—came into being before all things, so that anything might be in anything. In fact, in every creature the universe is the creature; consequently each creature receives all, so that in any creature all creatures are found in a relative way. Since all creatures are finite, no creature could be all things in act; but all things are contracted in order to form each creature. If, then, all things are in all, it is clear that all is prior to the individual; and all here does not signify plurality, for prior to the individual there is no plurality. For that reason all without plurality has preceded the individual in the order of nature with the consequence that in any actual individual there is not more than one: all without plurality is that one.

Only by way of contraction is the universe in things; in fact it is restricted by each actually existing thing to be actually what each thing is. Everything actually existing is in God, for He is the act of all. Act means perfection and the realization of what was possible. Since the universe restricted is in each actually existing individual, then evidently God, Who is in the universe, is in every individual and every individual actually existing is, like the universe, immediately in God. To say that 'everything is in everything' is the same as saying that God, by the intermediary of the universe, is in all things and that the universe, by the intermediary of all things, is in God. How God is without any diversity in all, since everything is everything, and how all is in God, because all is in all, are truths of a very high order which are clearly understood by keen minds. The universe is in each individual in such a way that each individual is in it, with the result that in each individual the universe is by contraction what the particular individual is; and every individual in the universe is the universe, though the universe is in each individual in a different way and each thing is in the universe in a different way.

Here is an example: The infinite line is clearly a line, a triangle, a circle and a sphere; but a finite line receives its existence from the infinite line, and the infinite line is all that the finite line is. All, therefore, that is identified with the infinite line—line, triangle and the others—is also found identified with the finite line. Every figure in the finite line is the line itself; but that does not mean that the triangle or circle or sphere is actually present in it. That everything is in everything does not imply actual presence, for the actual unity of the thing would be destroyed by such a plurality; but the triangle in the line is the line, the circle in the line is the line, and so on. To note that a line can only actually exist in a body—a point to be proved elsewhere—helps you to see this more clearly. No one doubts that in a body with length, breadth and depth all the figures are virtually contained. So in an actual line all the figures are actually the line itself, and in a triangle all are the triangle and so on. In a stone all is stone, in the vegetative soul all is soul, in life all is life, in a sense all is that sense, in sight all is sight, in hearing all is hearing, in the imagination all is imagination, in reason all is reason, in the understanding all is understanding, in God all is God. From that you see how the unity of things or the universe exists in plurality and conversely how plurality exists in unity.

You will also see on closer study how each individual in actual existence is at peace, for all in the individual is the individual and the individual in God is God; and there appears the wonderful unity of things, the admirable equality and the most remarkable connection, by which all is in all. In this we see the one source of the connection and diversity of things. An individual could not be actually all things, for it would be God, and therefore all things would be actualized in it in the way in which they can exist as individual natures. Nor can any two things be absolutely equal, as we proved above when we saw that all things were made in varying degrees of being—like the being which could not possess all at once the perfection of incorruptibility and was made to exist without corruption in temporal succession. Consequently, all things are what they are, because they could not be otherwise nor better.

Without any conflict, therefore, all is in each, because one degree of being cannot exist without another; e.g. in the body one member helps another and all the members are harmoniously united in the body. Since the eye cannot in act be the hand, foot and all the other members, it is content to be the eye, as the foot is content to be the foot; and all the members help one another, so that each is what it is in the best way possible. The hand is not in the eye, nor is the foot, but in the eye they are the eye, in as much as the eye itself is immediately in man; in this way, too, all the members are in the foot, in-so-far as the foot is immediately in man. The result is that any member through any other is immediately in man; and just as the whole is in its parts—through being in anyone it is in every other—so man, as a whole, is in every member through being in any one.

If you were to think of humanity as an absolute, immutable, illimitable being, and of man as a being in whom absolute humanity exists in an absolute way though contracted by him to the humanity which man is, then you might compare the absolute humanity to God and the contracted to the universe. Absolute humanity is found in man first and foremost and then in each member or part; contracted humanity is the eye in the eye, the heart in the heart and so on of the others, so that by contraction each is in each. Besides supplying us with the comparison of God and the world, our hypothesis is an illustration of all we have dealt with in the last two chapters and of much that is to follow.

CHAPTER VI. THE UNIVERSE—ITS UNITY AND DEGREES OF DEVELOPMENT

IN THE PREVIOUS CHAPTERS WE HAVE DISCOVERED, though it is above our understanding, that the universe or world is one, that its unity is restricted by plurality and, as a result, that its unity consists in a plurality. The unity of the universe proceeds from absolute unity, so that absolute unity is the first unity, and unity of the universe—a unity in plurality —is the second. In *De Coniecturis* we shall see that the second unity is tenfold, for it comprises the ten predicaments; and for that reason, the unity of the universe, which is the second unity, will be a tenfold restrictive development of the first absolute and simple unity. Since there is no number above it, ten is a number that embraces all things; in consequence, the multiplicity of all things finite is enfolded in the tenfold unity of the universe. Because it is in all as the finite principle of all, the unity of the universe is the root of all, as ten is the square root of a hundred and the cube root of a thousand. From this root there arises immediately, as it were, the square as a third unity and then the cube as a fourth and last unity. The third unity—the century—is the first development of the unity of the universe; the fourth unity—the millennium—is its last development.

In this way we shall see that there are three universal unities, which descend by degrees to the individual, in which they are contracted to form the actual individual. The first absolute unity embraces all in an absolute fashion; the first contracted unity enfolds all in a finite manner. Order demands that absolute unity should be regarded as enfolding the first contracted unity, and through it all others; that the first contracted unity be regarded as embracing the second contracted unity and, through the second, the third; and that the second contracted unity be viewed as including the third, so that by means of it the individual is reached. The third contracted unity is really the fourth when we count from the first, and it is the last universal unity. From this it is clear how the universe is brought down through these stages to any individual.

The universe, therefore, may be compared in turn to the ten most general all-embracing categories, the genera and species. These form the universals according to their grades; and it is nature's order that they should exist in these grades prior to their being actually contracted to an individual. As the universe is contracted, then the only possible development of it is into genera, and the one development of genera is into species. Individuals, however, are actual and in them the universe exists by contraction.

This makes it clear that universals have no actual existence save by contraction. The Peripatetics were right in saying that outside things universals have no actual existence. Only the singular has actual existence, and in the singular the universal by contraction is the singular. Yet in the order of nature universals have a certain universal being, which can be restricted by the individual; but before this contraction they have no being other than that which they have in the order of nature: they are not in act, they have no subsistence of their own but by contraction their universal being subsists in an individual that actually exists. To make a comparison: the point, the line, the surface precede the solid in an order of progression, but it is only in the solid that they have actual existence. Like the universe, all universals are only actual when contracted. Yet they are not simply beings of reason, though they have no actual existence apart from individuals. They are like the line and the surface, which are not merely beings of reason, despite the fact that outside the solid they have not actual existence: they exist in the solid as universals exist in the individuals. As absolute being cannot be attributed to them, the intellect by abstraction gives them an existence outside things; it is that abstraction that is a being of reason. God is the entirely absolute universal. In *De Coniecturis* we shall see how universals exist in the intellect by abstraction, though possibly this is sufficiently clear from what we have already said. In the intellect they are the intellect and accordingly are contracted by it. The act of the intellect, which is most clear and penetrating, apprehends the contraction of the universals in itself and in others. Dogs, and other animals of the same species, are put in the one category because of the specific nature which is common to them; and that nature would have been contracted to the individuals, even if the intellect of Plato had not created the species for them from a comparison of their resemblances. As far as its operation is concerned, understanding presupposes being and life, for it cannot by its act give being or life or understanding; but, with regard to the things understood, the understanding of the intellect itself presupposes being, life and understanding similar in nature. In consequence, the universals which it forms from comparisons are in the likeness of the universals contracted in individuals; and these universals have their contracted existence in the intellect itself prior to its development of them—through their individuating notes—by its operation, which is the act of understanding. Only that which is already in the intellect and by contraction is the intellect can be understood. By the act of understanding, therefore, it develops by means of similar characteristics and properties a world of resemblances which exists in it by contraction.

The question of the unity of the universe and its contracted existence in individuals has now had ample treatment. Let us add something about the trinity of the universe.

CHAPTER VII. THE TRINITY OF THE UNIVERSE

SUFFICIENT WAS SAID IN THE FIRST BOOK TO establish that the absolute unity is necessarily threefold, not by contraction but absolutely; in fact, the sole absolute unity is the Trinity, which by finite minds is grasped in a certain correlation. The contracted absolute unity, even in its unity, is also threefold; but it is by contraction it is threefold, so that its unity is in a trinity in the same way as the whole by contraction is in its parts. The Trinity, on the other hand, is unity absolutely, for there is not in God any contraction of the unity in the Trinity; it is not as the whole is in its parts or the universal in the individuals; but the unity is itself the Trinity. On that account any one of the Persons is unity itself; and because unity is the Trinity, one Person is not another. In the universe, of course, there can be nothing like that. It follows then that those three correlations, which are called Persons in God, co-exist actually and necessarily in unity.

These points demand our keen attention. In God so great is the perfection of the unity, which is the Trinity, that the Father is actually God, the Son actually God and the Holy Ghost actually God; the Son and the Holy Spirit are actually in the Father, the Son and the Father in the Holy Spirit, the Father and the Holy Spirit in the Son. Nothing of this sort can exist in the universe, in which correlations subsist per se only conjointly; in consequence, no one individual can be the universe; nor is one actually in the others, but all—in-so-far as their finite nature permits—are so perfectly reduced to one another that from them is formed the universe; and without that trinity the unity of the universe would be impossible. For contraction is impossible without a limitable object, a limiting principle and a connection. The connection is established by the common act of the other two.

Contractibility implies a certain possibility, which comes down from the creative unity in the Divine Persons, as otherness comes from unity. When considered from its beginning, it means the ability to change and be different. In fact, possibility evidently precedes everything, for how could anything at all exist if it had not been possible? Possibility, then, descends from eternal unity.

The limiting principle descends from the equality of unity, for it sets a limit to the possibility of the limitable object. Really the equality of unity and the equality of being are one, for being and unity are convertible. The limiting principle by contraction brings possibility to being in one form or another, and for that reason it is correctly maintained that the limiting principle descends from the equality of being, which is the Word of God. The Word, by means of the limiting principle, inevitably gives determination to possibility, for the Word is the motive, archetype and the essence of things. That is why by some matter has been called Possibility and the limiting principle the Form or Soul of the world; others have referred to the latter as Fate (fatum in substantia); others, like the Platonists, have called it the Universal Necessity, because it descends from absolute necessity to become a contracted necessity and contracted form, in which all forms are truly found. But we shall speak of this later.

Finally there is the connection of the limiting principle and the limitable object, of matter and form, of possibility and the necessity of the universe, which is actually brought about by the spirit of love uniting them through a certain movement. Some habitually refer to this connection as Possibility determined, for the union of the determining form and the determinable matter reduces possible being to an individual existing in act. It is clear that this connection descends from the Holy Spirit who is the Infinite Connection.

The unity of the universe, therefore, is threefold; it arises from possibility, the necessity of the universe and the connection or, in other words, from potency, act and the nexus. From this we get four universal modes of being. (1) The mode of being called absolute necessity, namely God, who is the form of forms, the being of beings, the reason or quiddity of things; and in this mode all things in God are absolute necessity itself. (2) The mode of being which things have in the necessity of the universe, where the forms of things, true in themselves, exist with the natural distinction and order that they have in the mind. Whether this is so or not we shall see later. (3) The mode of being enjoyed by things as individuals, which is possibility actually determined. (4) The lowest mode of being is that of possible being, which is absolute possibility.

The last three of these modes of being exist in the one universe which is the contracted maximum; and from these there arises one universal mode of being, for without them the existence of anything is impossible. I speak of 'modes of being', for the universal mode of being is not one composed, as it were, of three parts in the same way as a house is composed of foundation, walls and roof; rather it is made up of modes of being; as the rose, which was potential in its rose-tree in winter and becomes actual in summer, has passed from the mode of being which is possibility, to the mode which is actual determination. From this it is clear that there is (*a*) a mode of being which is possibility, (*b*) a mode which is necessity, (*c*) a mode that is actual determination. As existence is impossible without these and as they are incapable of actually existing separately, the one universal mode of being arises from the three of them.

CHAPTER VIII. POSSIBILITY OR MATTER OF THE UNIVERSE

LET US EXAMINE IN SOME LITTLE DETAIL THE THREE modes of being of which we have just spoken, so that we may here show, in substance at least, what it is that makes our ignorance learned. We will begin by studying possibility. The ancient philosophers have spoken a good deal on this subject and unanimously accepted the axiom: ex nihilo nihil fit. They admitted, in consequence, that the possibility of being all things was absolute, eternal and embraced all things as possibles. It was by reasoning from the contrary, as from Absolute Necessity, that they came to form an idea of this possibility or matter, just as through abstraction of the forma corporeitatis from body an idea of body is obtained. How can matter be intelligible if it has no form? It was only through ignorance, therefore, that they arrived at this idea of matter. Matter, they said, was by nature prior to all things, so that it never was true to say 'God exists' without its being equally true to say 'Absolute Possibility' exists; but, since it is from God, they did not assert that matter was co-eternal with Him. For them it was in possibility all things, whilst in act it was none of all the things it could be; though no thing in particular, it was not yet nothing; it was neither one nor many, neither this nor that, neither a substance nor an accident.

Since it was completely formless, Platonists referred to it as 'carentia'; and from the fact that it lacks forms arises its appetite for them, which makes it ready to accept whatever form is imposed on it by necessity, or whatever tends to bring it into the order of actuality; it is like wax in the hand of him who is about to make something from it. The fact that it is formless is due to its 'carentia' and its appetite; and its formlessness links the two in such a way that absolute possibility results as a simple trinity—simple, since 'carentia', aptitude and formlessness cannot be regarded as its parts, for that would then imply that something preceded absolute possibility, which is absurd. For that reason they are modes, without which absolute possibility would not be absolute. In fact it is contingently that 'carentia' is found in possibility, for it is through its not having the form which it could have that it is said to be lacking; hence the term 'carentia'. On the other hand, formlessness is a sort of form of possibility, and possibility, according to the Platonists, is the matter, so to speak, of forms. For the soul of the world is united to matter in compliance with that which they called the 'vegetable appetite'. Thus, by the union of the soul of the world and possibility, that formless vegetability is brought into actuality as the vegetative soul, by a movement descending from the soul of the world and the aptitude to move of possibility or vegetability. On that account they spoke of this formlessness as a sort of matter of forms, which, to be actualized, has to receive a sensitive, rational and intellectual form.

Hermes, accordingly, said ὕλη was the nurse of bodies and formlessness the nurse of souls; and some of us have maintained that chaos naturally preceded the world as the possibility of things; and that in that chaos there was the formless spirit in which all souls exist in a state of possibility.

The ancient Stoics were thus led to assert that in possibility all forms, though latent, are actual; they are made to appear by the removal of the covering, just as from a piece of wood a spoon is made merely by the cutting away of parts.

On the other hand, the Peripatetics held that in matter the forms only existed as possibles and became actual through the action of an efficient cause. It is, therefore, more correct to say that forms owe their origin not only to possibility but also to the action of an efficient cause, for it is clear that to cut pieces from a block of wood, in order to make a statue of it, is to give it some form. If a craftsman cannot make a wooden box from stone, the reason lies in the entire unsuitability of the material; if one who is not a craftsman cannot make it from wood, the fault is in the efficient cause. Matter and an efficient cause are, therefore, necessary. Forms, then, are in matter as possibles in some way; their actualization remains dependent upon an efficient cause.

In consequence, they have said that all things are contained potentially in absolute possibility. The boundless infinite character of absolute possibility arises at once from its having no form, and from its aptitude for all forms; e.g. the possible forms that may be given to a piece of wax are limitless: the form of a lion, hare or anything at all. Yet it is an infinity that is the opposite of God's, for it is through want that it is infinite, whereas God's infinity is by abundance, since in God all things are God in act. The conclusion, then, of those who have discussed absolute possibility is that the infinity of matter is privative and that of God negative.

We, on the contrary, have discovered, through the ignorance that enlightens, that it would be impossible for possibility to be absolute. Our reason is this, that among possibles nothing can be less than absolute possibility, for, even on the admission of authors, that comes nearest to non-being. Therefore, in things which are capable of degrees we would have reached a minimum and a maximum, which is absurd. Absolute possibility, in consequence, in God is God and outside Him there can be no question of absolute possibility; for all, apart from God, is necessarily limited, so that no thing could be found which is absolute possibility. If, in fact, different beings of the world are such that the potentialities of one are greater than those of another, yet a simple, absolute maximum and minimum does not exist among them; but this is so with the beings of the world; therefore, it is evident that it must be denied that possibility is absolute.

All possibility consequently is limited, and its limitation comes from act, so that there can be no question of pure possibility or possibility that is not determined in some way by some act or other; nor can the aptitude of possibility be infinite and absolute, devoid of all limitation. For God is only the cause of act since He is Infinite Act; but possibility has only contingent being. How, then, would its contingency be explained, if possibility were absolute? The contingency of possibility arises from this, that the First Being cannot produce a being which is wholly and simply absolute act. Act, therefore, receives a limitation from possibility, so that it has no absolute existence save in potency, whilst possibility can have no absolute existence save when it is limited by act.

We find that one thing is more in act, another more in potency; yet, these differences and degrees do exist without ever reaching an absolute maximum and absolute minimum, for the maximum and the minimum act are identified with the maximum and the minimum potency; they are the Absolute Maximum properly so-called, as we saw in the First Book.

In addition, if the possibility of things were not limited, there could be no rational explanation of anything, but all would be due to chance, as Epicurus wrongly maintained. In fact, the possibility of this world was contracted to the aptitude to be this world, and that necessarily was the reason why this world from being possible was brought into actual existence. The aptitude, then, of the possibility was limited and not absolute. The same, too, must be said of the earth, the sun and the rest, since, for them also, there would have been no greater reason for their coming into actuality rather than not, unless in some limited possible form they had been latent in matter.

It follows, then, that, since God is infinite, He could, in consequence, have created the world infinite; yet since possibility is of necessity limited and its aptitude neither completely absolute nor infinite, the world could not, by reason of its possible being, be actually infinite, greater, or in any way other than it is. The limitation of possibility comes from act and act proceeds from the Infinite Act. Since, therefore, the limitation of possibility is from God, and the limitation of the act is due to contingency, it follows that the world, necessarily limited through contingency, is finite. Thus it is evident, from our knowledge of possibility, how the limited maximum comes from the necessarily limited possibility; and this limitation is due to act, not to contingency. Our conclusion is that there is a rational explanation and necessary cause of the universe's being finite, which means that the world—merely a finite being —necessarily owes its existence to God, for He is the Absolute Maximum.

We must study this more closely. Absolute possibility is God; if we consider the world as it is in absolute possibility, we are considering it as it is in God, and then it is eternity itself; if we consider it as it is in limited possibility, then possibility is only prior by nature to the world; that limited possibility is not eternity, nor is it co-eternal with God, but it descends from eternity, as the limited from the absolute; and they are infinitely distant from one another.

In accord with the rules of enlightened ignorance we must

confine ourselves to these remarks on potency or possibility or matter. How possibility gradually proceeds to act must be left for treatment in *De Coniecturis*.

CHAPTER IX. THE SOUL OR FORM OF THE UNIVERSE

ALL PHILOSOPHERS GRANT THAT POSSIBLE BEING can only be made actual by a being that is in act; nothing, in fact, is capable of bringing itself into the actual order, for that would involve its being cause of itself, or its being actual before it existed. They have, in consequence, maintained that possibility passes to actuality because an agent has willed that it should do so, so that its becoming actual is not a matter of chance but is the outcome of an order of reason.

Different names have been given to this superior agent: Mind, Intelligence, Soul of the World, Fate; and some, like the Platonists, have called it Universal Necessity, for it was it, they thought, that necessarily determined possibility to be now in the actual order what by nature it was before in the possible order. They said that the forms of things existed in that Mind as ideas in much the same way as they are found in matter as possibles. Possessing the truth of the forms with all that goes with them, Universal Necessity, they asserted, caused the heavens to move according to the natural order; by the instrumentality of the movement it brought possibility to a state of actualization, which conformed as perfectly as possible with the concept of truth in the Mind. The form as it is in matter is, according to these philosophers, through that operation of the mind and by means of that movement, an image of the true ideal form; it is, in consequence, not the true form but is similar to it. The conclusion of the Platonists was that prior to existing in things the true forms existed in the Soul of the World by a priority not of time but of nature. Rejecting this opinion, the Peripatetics state that the only existence forms have is in matter and in the mind by abstraction; and abstraction, it is evident, is made once the thing has existed. That distinct exemplars of this sort did exist in the Universal Necessity was defended by the Platonists; they were multiple in correspondence with the order of nature and they were from the one Infinite Reason in which all things are one. They did not mean thereby that these exemplars were created by the Infinite Reason but merely that they descend in such a way that it was never true to say 'God Exists' without it being equally true to say 'The Soul of the World exists'. For them the Soul of the World is an unfolding of the mind of God, so that all the things which in God are one exemplar, are in the Soul of the World multiple and distinct; and they went on to say that God by nature was prior to the Universal Necessity, that the Soul of the World by nature preceded the movement, that the movement as instrument preceded the development of things in time. The result, for them, was that those things which have a true existence in the Soul and a possible existence in matter were in time developed by movement. This development in time follows the order of nature which is in the Soul of the World and is called Fate (fatum in substantia); and its development in time is called destiny by most, because in effect it derives from Fate (fatum in substantia).

Thus, according to them, when we speak of the intelligible world we are referring to its mode of being in the Soul of the World; when we speak of the sensible world we are referring to its actual mode of being which is developed, as already said, by the actualization of possibility through determination. Yet they maintained that the forms, as they exist in matter and as they are in the Soul of the World, are not really distinct from one another; only their mode of being differs: in the Soul of the

World they have a true substantial existence, whereas in matter they are shadowy resemblances without their original clarity. They added that the intellect alone is able to reach the true forms; reason, imagination and sense grasp only the images in-so-far as they are forms immersed in matter; and that is why they give us mere conjecture, and not the truth, about anything.

They were of opinion that all movement came from this Soul of the World, which, they said, was entire in the whole and entire in each part of the world, though its influence is not the same in different parts; just as with the rational soul, which is entire in the whole and in each part of man, and yet its activity in the hairs and the heart is not the same. For that reason they argued that all souls, whether in bodies or not, were contained in the Soul of the World, for it is diffused throughout the entire universe; not in the sense that one part was here and another there, since it is simple and indivisible, but that it is entire in the earth, which, by its power, is held together, entire in a stone where the function is to hold the parts united, entire in water, entire in trees, entire in each thing. The Soul of the World is the first circular development (the Divine Mind being, as it were, a central point which the Soul of the World develops in the form of a circle); it is also by nature the totality of all things in the order of time. This plurality and unity (discretio et ordo) led them to refer to the Soul of the World as 'self-moving number' and to say that identity and diversity were one in it. It was also their opinion that number alone distinguished it from the soul of man; just as the human soul is related to man, so the soul of the World stands to the universe, for it was their belief that all souls had their origin in it and returned to it as their end, should their misdeeds not stand in their way.

This Platonic theory was acceptable to many Christians. Especially from the fact that in God there is no distinction, no 'otherness', and from the fact that the essence of stone is distinct from the essence of man, they argued that these distinct essences, exemplars of the different things that exist, must have an existence posterior to God and prior to the things themselves, since reason precedes the thing, particularly in the Mind of Him who governs the worlds; and such distinct essences as these are the indestructible ideas of things existing in the Soul of the World. They even held that the Soul of the World and the ideas of all things were so identified that all the ideas in it form its substance, though on their own admission this is far from easy to grasp and explain.

In defence of their opinion they appeal to the Scriptures; e.g. 'God said: let there be light, and there was light'. Now, why should He have said 'Let there be light', if by nature light did not exist in truth beforehand? And if it had not a prior existence of this kind, why should it have been called light rather than anything else, once it was created in time? They bring forward a number of similar texts in confirmation of their theory.

Whilst granting that the work of nature is the work of an intelligence, the Peripatetics refuse to admit the existence of these exemplars; if, for them, that intelligence is not God, I certainly think they are wrong. In fact, if in that intelligence there is no idea, what purpose could be assigned for its movement? If there is the idea of the thing which has to be given existence in time that idea is the reason for the movement; and such an idea could not be abstracted from the thing, which does not yet exist in time. If, therefore, there is an idea which is not obtained by abstraction, then that certainly is the idea which, instead of being obtained from the things, is their exemplar, as the Platonists maintain. For the Platonists, in consequence, the reasons or essences of things, though distinct from one another, were identified with the Intelligence Itself, and formed, in fact, one simple Intelligence which contained in itself all the essences; e.g. the essence of man and the essence of stone are two distinct essences; but humanity, which man participates as a white object participates whiteness, has an ideal existence in the intelligence in conformity with the nature of the intelligence, whereas in the thing itself it has a real existence. It has no other being than that. There is no question, then, of two humanities: the humanity of Plato and humanity enjoying a separate or distinct existence; the modes of being are different but it is one and the same being whose existence in the intelligence is prior—not in time but by nature—to its existence in matter, just as reason is naturally prior to the thing.

The arguments of the Platonists were certainly to the point, and well founded. Aristotle's refutation of them was far from well founded, for he directed his attack not so much against the substance of their teaching, as its verbal expression. We will see in the light of that ignorance that is learning on which side truth is. For we have proved that the Simple Maximum is beyond our grasp; that, in consequence, there is no absolute potency or absolute form or act which is not God; that apart from God every being is limited; that there is one sole form of forms, one sole truth of truths and in the Maximum the truth of the circle is not different from that of the quadrangle. It is only therefore in their finite state that the forms of things are distinct; in the absolute they are not many and distinct but one; and that one is the Word of God. The Soul of the World, therefore, necessarily co-exists with matter from which it receives a limitation; it does not exist as a mind separated or separable from things. If we regard the mind as free of all potentiality, then we are thinking of the Divine mind, for it alone is pure act. A plurality of distinct exemplars is then absurd, for each would be to the objects modelled on it the infinitely true exemplar; but infinite truth can only be one. One infinite exemplar is all that is needed and one alone suffices. In it all things are arranged, so to speak, in order, and all essences, however distinct, are most adequately unified in it, so that without any degree at all of diversity or difference the infinite essence itself is the essence of the perfect circle, the essence of the quadrangle, and the essence of all the other figures, as can be understood from the example of the infinite line.

When we consider the diversity of things we are at a loss to see how the unique absolutely simple essence of all things is also the distinct essence of particular things; yet we know that it must be so, for our ignorance that is learning has shown us that in God identity is diversity. Perceiving that the diversity of the essences of all things is most truly a fact, we grasp, from the absolute truth of this fact, the one absolutely true essence of all things, which is Infinite Truth itself. When we say, there-fore, that God has created distinct essences—the essence of man is different from the essence of stone—these distinctions are true in reference to things but not with reference to the Creator. We have, for example, the same thing in numbers where the ternary, which in itself is one, is the absolutely simple essence or reason not susceptible of degrees; diversity or distinction exists in-so-far as that absolutely simple essence is in relationship with the different things. The essence of the trinity of angles in a triangle, the essence of matter, of form and of the composite in a substance are all different; so, too, are the essences of mother, father and son, or of three men and three asses, all different. The Platonists, then, were wrong in regarding Universal Necessity as a Mind inferior to the Creator; it is the Word, the Son equal to the Father in the Deity, to Whom is given the name Logos or Reason because He is the Reason why all things exist. So the Platonists' theory about the images of forms has to be completely discounted, for there is but one infinite form of forms and of it all forms are images, as we have already remarked.

It is necessary, therefore, for us to have a keen grasp of these points. The Soul of the World has, in fact, to be regarded as a universal form which contains within itself all the forms; yet it has only a contracted actual existence in things and in each thing it is the contracted form of the thing, as we said previously of the universe. Therefore the efficient and formal and final cause of all is God, who in the one Word creates all things however different they be; and every creature owes its existence to this creative act of God and for that reason is finite. Between it and the Creator there is an infinity. God alone is Absolute, all else is finite.

Thus between the Absolute and the finite there is no mean, as was imagined by those who regarded the Soul of the World as the Mind whose existence was posterior to God's but prior to the existence of the finite world. Only if the Soul is looked upon as something absolute, in which all the forms of things are actual, may God be called the Soul and Mind of the World. It was because philosophers had not sufficiently clear ideas on the Word of God and the Absolute Maximum that they thought to see in the development of Absolute Necessity a mind, soul and necessity that was in no way limited.

Forms, therefore, are only actual in the Word where they are the Word itself and in things where they are finite. Forms of a created intellectual nature are, by reason of their intellectual nature, more independent; yet they are none the less finite, for example intellects, whose operation is to know by concepts, as Aristotle says. Of this we will have something to say in *De Coniecturis*. Our study here of the Soul of the World should suffice.

CHAPTER X. SPIRIT OF THE UNIVERSE

SOME HAVE THOUGHT THAT THE MOVEMENT, BY WHICH the connection of matter and form is effected, is a spirit intermediary between matter and form and diffused throughout the firmament, the planets and things of earth.

Because the movement of the firmament was not a rotation but went simply from east to west they called it Atropos, the Unalterable, as it were; because the planets rotated and had a movement from west to east in opposition to the firmament they named it Clotho, i.e. rotation; and lastly, because the things of earth are governed by chance they named it Lachesis or Fate.

The movement of the planets develops, as it were, from the first movement and the movement of temporal and earthly things is a development of the movement of the planets. Like the harvest in the seed, the causes of events are latent in things of earth, which has led them to conclude that those things which are contained, as in a ball of thread, in the Soul of the World are unwound and given extension by movement of this kind. Philosophers exemplified this from the sculptor who wishes to make a statue in stone. In the mind of the sculptor there exists the idea of the form of the statue and he produces, by the tools which he moves, the actual form of the statue modelled on his idea; in a similar way they thought the Mind or Soul of the World had within it the exemplars of things, which were materialized by movement. They held that this movement was diffused throughout all things as the Soul of the World. Much as chance (fatum) is a development in act and deed of Fate (fatum in substantia), so this movement, they maintained, in the firmament, the planets and the things of earth is a development of Fate (fatum in substantia), because by that very movement or spirit a thing's being is specifically determined.

They affirmed that this spirit of connection proceeds at once from matter and the Soul of the World. In fact, from the aptitude of matter to receive a form springs a desire: it desires a form as evil desires good and privation desires possession. Form, too, has a desire—a desire to be actualized; but since its existence cannot be absolute, for it is not its own being and it is not God, it descends in order to have a limited existence in matter.

In other words, whilst matter ascends towards being actual, form descends to limit, perfect and determine matter. Thus from the ascent and descent there arises the movement which connects the two of them. Potency and act are connected by means of this movement, for movement itself, which is the intermediary, springs from moveable matter and a formal mover.

This, then, is the finite spirit that is diffused throughout the entire universe and all its parts and to which is given the name nature. Nature, therefore, embraces, as it were, all things which owe their origin to movement. How this movement is reduced in due order and by degrees from the universal to the particular is illustrated by the following example. When I say 'God exists' that pronouncement is formed by a movement and according to a definite order; first I utter the letters, then the syllables, then the words and finally the sentence, though these orderly stages are not perceived by the ear. So, too, does movement descend by stages from the universal to the particular, where it is limited by the temporal or natural order. This movement or spirit descends from the Spirit of God who put all things in movement by movement itself. Just as, therefore, in a speaker there is a breath or spirit which proceeds from him and is formed into a sentence, as we have already said, so God, Who is a Spirit, is He from Whom all movement descends. Truth Himself tells us: 'It is not you who speak but the Spirit of your Father who speaks in you.' The same has to be said of all other movements and operations.

This created spirit, then, is the spirit without which there is no unity, without which nothing can subsist. It fills the whole earth; by it the entire world and all it contains are naturally what they are connectedly, so that by means of this spirit potency is in act and act, through it, is in potency. This is the movement of a love that links all in one with the result that all things form one universe. All things, in fact, are moved individually to be precisely what they are; and they would not be another thing equally as well, for they are what they are in the best possible way. Yet, at the same time, in its own proper way each thing shares in and limits the movement of all others either mediately or immediately: the elements share in and limit the movement of the heavens and the elements and all the members share in and limit the movement of the heart, with the result that the universe is a unity. By this movement things exist in the best way possible; and the purpose of the movement is their own preservation, or the preservation of their species through the union of the sexes, for, though in the individuals the sexes are defined and separate, in nature, in which the movement exists, they are united.

In consequence, it is impossible to have a movement that would be simply the greatest for it and rest would coincide. No movement, therefore, is absolute, for absolute movement is rest. It is God, and in Him all movements are contained. Just as possibility is contained in the Absolute Possibility, which is the Eternal God, and every form and act in the Absolute Form which is the Word of the Father and Son of God, so every movement that connects and every relation and harmony that unites is in the absolute connection of the Holy Spirit, so that there is but one principle of all things, God. In Him and through Him all things exist in a triune unity as finite images, in the finite world, of the Trinity, which they resemble more or less according to their degrees of being. In intellectual natures, as a result, we find a degree of potency, act and movement of connection, and here to move is to understand; in corporeal things we have another degree: matter, form and connection, and here to move is to exist; but we will deal with this in another place. For the moment we have said enough about the trinity of the universe.

CHAPTER XI. COROLLARIES OF MOVEMENT

THE FACT THAT THE IGNORANCE WHICH IS LEARN-ing has shown the truth of the foregoing doctrine will perhaps be a surprise to those who had not heard of such teaching before. By it we now know that the universe is a trinity; that there is not a being in the universe which is not a unity composed of potency, act and the movement connecting them and that none of these three is capable of absolute subsistence without the others, with the result that they are necessarily found in all things in the greatest diversity of degrees— in degrees so different that it is impossible to find in the universe two beings perfectly equal in all things. Consequently, once we have taken the different movements of the stars (orbium) into account, we see that it is impossible for the motor of the world to have the material earth, air, fire or anything else for a fixed, immovable centre. In movement there is no absolute minimum, like a fixed centre, since necessarily the minimum and the maximum are identical.

Therefore the centre and the circumference are identical. Now the world has no circumference. It would certainly have a circumference if it had a centre, in which case it would contain within itself its own beginning and end; and that would mean that there was some other thing which imposed a limit to the world—another being existing in space outside the world. All of these conclusions are false. Since, then, the world cannot be enclosed within a material circumference and centre, it is unintelligible without God as its centre and circumference. It is not infinite, yet it cannot be conceived as finite, since there are no limits within which it is enclosed.

The earth, which cannot be the centre, must in some way be in motion; in fact, its movement even must be such that it could be infinitely less. Just as the earth is not the centre of the world, so the circumference of the world is not the sphere of the fixed stars, despite the fact that by comparison the earth seems nearer the centre and heaven nearer the circumference. The earth, then, is not the centre of the eighth or any other sphere, and the appearance above the horizon of the six stars is no proof that the earth is at the centre of the eighth sphere. If even at some distance from the centre it were revolving on its axis through the poles, in such a way that one part would be facing upwards towards one pole and the other part facing downwards towards the other pole, then, it is evident, that to men as distant from the poles as the horizon only half of the sphere would be visible. Further, the centre itself of the world is no more within than outside the earth; and this earth of ours has no centre nor has any other sphere a centre. Since the centre is a point equidistant from the circumference, and since it is impossible to have a sphere or circle so perfect that a more perfect one could not be given, it clearly follows that a centre could always be found that is truer and more exact than any given centre. Only in God are we able to find a centre which is with perfect precision equidistant from all points, for He alone is infinite equality. God, ever to be blessed, is, therefore, the centre of the world: He it is who is centre of the earth, of all spheres and of all things in the world; and at the same time He is the infinite circumference of all.

In addition, in the heavens there are no fixed, immovable poles, though the heaven of the fixed stars seems to move in describing circles smaller and smaller in magnitude—smaller than the equinoctial colures or the equinoctial minores [circulos minores] quam coluros [aut] aequinoctialem); and so on for the intermediaries. Necessarily all parts of the heavens are in movement, though their movement is not uniform by comparison with the circles that the stars in their movement describe. That explains why certain stars seem to describe the maximum circle, whilst others seem to describe the minimum; but there is not a star which does not describe a circle. It is clear that a centre equidistant from the poles cannot be found, for the simple reason that there is no fixed pole on the sphere. In consequence, in the eighth sphere there is not a star which in its revolution describes the maximum circle, for that would necessarily mean that it was equidistant from the poles; but the poles do not exist. It follows also that there is no star which describes the minimum circle.

The poles, therefore, of the spheres and the centre coincide so that there is no centre but the pole, which is God ever to be blessed. It is only by reference to a fixed point—poles or centres —that we are able to detect movement, and we take such fixed points for granted in our measurements of movements. By reason of these assumptions which we make we find ourselves involved in error on all points, and, because we do not question the notions the ancients had about centres, poles and measurements, we are puzzled when we discover that the stars are not in the position indicated by their system.

It is evident from the foregoing that the earth is in movement. We have learned from the movement of a comet that the elements of air and fire are in movement and that the moon is moved less from east to west than Mercury or Venus or the sun; and so on by degrees. It follows, then, that the earth itself is moved least of all. In its movement, however, the earth does not, like a star, describe the minimum circle around a centre or pole; nor does the eighth sphere describe the maximum circle, as we have just proved.

As a keen observer, then, consider that just as the stars moved around imaginary poles on the eighth sphere, so, by imagining there is a pole where the centre is supposed to be, the earth, moon and planets move like stars around this pole at a distance from it, and with different movements. The earth, therefore, is in movement and, though as a star it may be nearer the central pole, it does not describe in its movement the minimum circle, as we have shown. In addition, though it may seem otherwise to us, neither the sun nor the moon nor the earth, nor any sphere can describe a true circle by its movement, since its movement is not on a fixed point. A given circle cannot be so true that a truer one cannot be found; and the movement of a sphere at one moment is never precisely equal to its movement at another, nor does it ever describe two circles similar and equal, even if from appearances the opposite may seem true.

If you really wish to understand something of what we have just said about the movement of the universe, you must regard the centre and the poles as coincident, using the help of your imagination as much as possible. Suppose one person were on the earth and under the arctic pole and that another were on the arctic pole; to him on the earth the pole would seem at the zenith, whereas to the person on the pole the centre would appear at the zenith. And just as the antipodes have the heavens above them as we have, so the earth would appear at the zenith to those on both poles; and no matter where a person were he would believe he was at the centre. Take, then, all these various images you have formed and merge them in one, so that the centre becomes the zenith and vice versa; and your intellect, which is aided so much by the ignorance that is learning, then sees the impossibility of comprehending the world, its movement and form, for it will appear as a wheel in a wheel, a sphere in a sphere without a centre or circumference anywhere, as has been said.

CHAPTER XII. CONDITIONS OF THE EARTH

THE ANCIENT PHILOSOPHERS DID NOT REACH these truths we have just stated, because they lacked learned ignorance. It is now evident that this earth really moves though to us it seems stationary. In fact, it is only by reference to something fixed that we detect the movement of anything. How would a person know that a ship was in movement, if, from the ship in the middle of the river, the banks were invisible to him and he was ignorant of the fact that water flows? Therein we have the reason why every man, whether he be on earth, in the sun or on another planet, always has the impression that all other things are in movement whilst he himself is in a sort of immovable centre; he will certainly always choose poles which will vary accordingly as his place of existence is the sun, the earth, the moon, Mars, etc. In consequence, there will be a machina mundi whose centre, so to speak, is everywhere, whose circumference is nowhere, for God is its circumference and centre and He is everywhere and nowhere.

Even the earth is not a sphere as some have maintained, though it is inclined to be spherical. The figure of the world, like its movement, is limited in its parts; and when an infinite line is thought of as limited in such a way that, as limited, it is incapable of greater perfection or extension, then it is circular, for there beginning and end are coincident. Circular movement, therefore, is the more perfect, from which it follows that the more perfect solid figure is the sphere. Therefore the movement of any part is for the perfection of the whole; e.g. heavy bodies move towards the earth, light things upwards, earth towards earth, water to water, air to air, fire to fire; and in its movement the whole tends as much as possible to become circular and every figure inclines to the spherical, as we perceive in the members of animals, in trees and in the heavens. One movement, in consequence, is more circular and more perfect than another; and figures differ in like manner.

The earth, then, is a stately and spherical figure whose movement is circular; but it could be more perfect. From what has just been said it is clear that in the world there is neither a maximum nor a minimum in perfections, movements and figures, so that it is untrue to say that this earth is the basest and lowest planet; if, in fact, it seems more central than the other planets of the world, it is also for that very reason nearer the pole, as was already said. The earth is not a comparative part of the world, nor is it an aliquot part of the world; for the world has neither a maximum nor a minimum and, in consequence, has neither a middle nor aliquot parts. With man or animal we have the same thing, for, though the hand of man seems to bear a relation to his body through its weight it is not an aliquot part of man; and the same assertion has to be made of magnitude and figure. Nor is the darkness of colour a proof of the earth's baseness; for the brightness of the sun, which is visible to us, would not be perceived by anyone who might be in the sun. Like the earth, the sun has its peculiar constitution. On examination the body of the sun is found to be disposed like this: nearer the centre there is a sort of earth, at the circumference a sort of fiery brightness and midway between them a kind of watery cloud and clearer air. Consequently if one were outside the region of fire, our earth at the circumference of the region would appear through the midst of the fire as a bright star, in much the same way as the sun appears brightest to us who are around the circumference of the solar region. Possibly the explanation of the moon's not appearing so bright lies in the fact that we are on the near side of its circumference towards the more central parts—in its watery region, as it were. It is for that reason that its light is not apparent, though it has its own light, which is visible to those existing on the extremities of its circumference; to us only the reflected light of the sun is visible. On that account, too, the moon's heat—the indubitable effect of its movement and greater in the circumference where the movement is greater —is not communicated to us like the sun's heat. Our earth, therefore, seems to lie between the region of the sun and the moon and through these it is influenced by other stars that are invisible to us, since we are outside their region. The regions of the stars that sparkle are the only ones we see.

The earth, then, is a brilliant star having a light, heat and influence distinctively its own and different from those of all other stars just as each star differs from every other in light, nature and influence. Each star communicates to another light and influence; but this communication is not the purpose of the stars, for all stars move and sparkle for one sole purpose: the realization of the best possible existence for them; and from that communication follows as a consequence. Likewise, light gives light not that I may see but it is of its very nature to give light; the communication of light takes place as a consequence when I use it for the purpose of seeing. God, ever to be blessed, has so created all things that whilst each thing strives to conserve its own being as a gift of God, it does so in participation with other things; e.g. the foot has only one purpose, viz. walking, but in carrying that out it is of service not only to the foot but to the eye, hands, body and the whole man. Similar examples of this are the eye and the other members; and the parts of the world equally exemplify it. Plato said the world was an animal. If, without his being immersed in it, you conceive God as its soul, much of what has been said will be clear to you.

Because the earth is smaller than the sun and is influenced by it is not a reason for calling it baser, for the entire region of the earth, which stretches to the circumference of fire, is great. From shadow and eclipses we know that the earth is smaller than the sun; yet despite that we do not know to what extent the region of the sun is greater or smaller than the region of the earth. It cannot be exactly equal to it, for no star can be equal to another. And the earth is not the smallest star, for eclipses have shown us that it is larger than the moon; and some say that it is larger even than Mercury, larger, perhaps, than all other stars. From size, therefore, no proof can be alleged of its baseness.

Even the influence exerted on it is not a proof of its imperfection; perhaps it, as a star, has a similar influence on the sun and its region, as already stated. We have no knowledge from experience of that influence, since we have no experience beyond that of our existence in the centre where the influences merge. Even if, in fact, we consider the earth as potency, the sun as its formal act or soul, and the moon as their connecting medium, the result would be the mutual relation of the influences of those stars situated within the one region (others like Mercury, Venus, etc., are above this region, according to the ancients and even some moderns); then the correlation of influence is clearly such that one could not exist without another. Likewise, in different degrees this influence, one and threefold, will be found in all. As regards these points, it is evidently impossible for man to discover whether the region of the earth is in degree more perfect or less perfect by comparison with the regions of the other stars such as the sun, moon and the others.

Nor can place furnish an argument for the earth's baseness. Life, as it exists here on earth in the form of men, animals and plants, is to be found, let us suppose, in a higher form in the solar and stellar regions. Rather than think that so many stars and parts of the heavens are uninhabited and that this earth of ours alone is peopled—and that with beings, perhaps, of an inferior type—we will suppose that in every region there are inhabitants, differing in nature by rank and all owing their origin to God, who is the centre and circumference of all stellar regions. Now, even if inhabitants of another kind should exist in the other stars, it seems inconceivable that, in the line of nature, anything more noble and perfect could be found than the intellectual nature that exists here on this earth and its region. The fact is that man has no longing for any other nature but desires only to be perfect in his own.

Were we to suppose that, for the realization of the plan of the universe, the whole region of the other inhabited stars stands in some relation of comparison, unknown to us, to the whole region of this earth; and that, in consequence, through the intermediary of the universal region a certain relationship springs up from both sides between the inhabitants of this earth or region and the inhabitants of the other stars—in the same way as through the intermediary of the hand there exists a relation of comparison between the particular joints of the fingers and the foot, and through the intermediary of the foot between the particular joints of the foot and the hand, so that all be suitably adapted to the whole animal; not even then with this supposition could we find a relation of comparison between those inhabitants of the other stars, of whatever nature they be, and the natives of this world.

For since that whole region is unknown to us, its inhabitants remain wholly unknown. To go no further than this earth:—animals of a given species unite to form a common home of the species and share the common characteristics of their habitat, knowing nothing of or caring nothing for strangers. Their idea of strangers, even if it reaches some kind of vocal expression, is wholly exterior and conjectural and, such as it is, conceivable only after lengthy experience. Of the inhabitants then of worlds other than our own we can know still less, having no standards by which to appraise them. It may be conjectured that in the area of the sun there exist solar beings, bright and enlightened intellectual denizens, and by nature more spiritual than such as may inhabit the moon—who are possibly lunatics—whilst those on earth are more gross and material. It may be supposed that those solar intelligences are highly actualized and little in potency, while the earth-denizens are much in potency and little in act, and the moon-dwellers betwixt and between.

We make these conjectures from a consideration of the fiery nature of the sun, the water and air elements in the moon and the weighty bulk of the earth. And we may make parallel surmise of other stellar areas that none of them lack inhabitants, as being each, like the world we live in, a particular area of one universe which contains as many such areas as there are uncountable stars. In these local areas (we may guess), so countless that only He who has created all things in number can enumerate them, the whole cosmos suffers a triple contraction in its downward fourfold progress.

Nor is the physical decay which we see upon the earth a convincing proof that our earth is vile. Given a single cosmos with the action and reaction of star upon star, we can never pronounce any one thing to be pure, irredeemable corruption. Stellar influences when focused upon an individual may sometimes fall away into its constituent elements, so that one or other mode of existence disappears; and therefore, it were better to regard corruption as different modes of being, and to pronounce with Virgil that there is no room for death anywhere. For death would appear to be no more than the resolution of a composite into its elements. And who shall say that such resolution occurs only upon this earth?

It has been asserted that there is a separate species on the earth to correspond with each one of the stars. Now if the earth provides in each species a focus for the action of each star, why may not a similar provision be made among other heavenly bodies that are subject to the action of their fellows? And who shall say that such stellar activity, now contracted in a composition, upon the resolution of that composition into its elements does not return whence it came; that the individual animal of a particular species upon the earth does not, when withdrawn from all stellar action, dissolve into its aboriginal matter, its form alone returning to that particular star from which that species derived actual being upon mother earth? Or that the form alone does not revert to the exemplar, the soul of the world, as say the Platonists, and the matter to the state of possibility? The energy which united them, the spirit of union that they receive from the movement of the stars, might, upon the maladjustment of organs or other cause of corruption, give place to a separatist movement and withdraw to the stars, while the form climbed above astral influence and the matter sank below it. Or who shall say that the forms of a particular area of creation do not come to rest in a higher form, say an intellectual one, and by its means attain the ultimate purpose of the universe? And as this purpose is attained in God by inferior forms by means of this intellectual one, so it itself is to rise to the circumference, which is God, while the body sinks to the centre where God also is, so that all movement may be Godward. Centre and circumference are one in God, and in Him at the right moment the centre-seeking body and circumference-tending soul shall be united. Meanwhile movement being stilled, not indeed all movement but such as makes for generation, these essential elements of the world, without which the world could not be, and, with the end of generation in time, possible matter shall be re-united with its form through the concurrence of the reviving energy of union.

These things, however, no man can know unless he be specially instructed by God. Doubtless, the God of infinite excellence has created all things for Himself and wills not that anything should perish of those things that He has made. Doubtless, also, He is the most bountiful rewarder of all who worship Him. But the manner of His present operation and of His bountifulness to come only God knows: for He is His own activity. Later I shall add a little more, as far as God gives me to understand, to what it must for the moment suffice to have touched upon in ignorance.

CHAPTER XIII. THE DIVINE DESIGN IN THE CREATION OF THE WORLD AND ITS CONSTITUENT PARTS IS WHOLLY ADMIRABLE

THAT THE VAST BULK, THE BEAUTY AND THE ordered adjustment of this visible world must fill us with amazement at the incomparable skill of its creator, goes without question among wise men. We have touched upon some examples of the astonishing creative skill of the divine mind. Let us now briefly add a word more, in admiration of the placing and mutual adjustment of the elements of creation.

When we measure the size and analyse the elements and study the behaviour of things, we make use of the sciences of arithmetic and geometry and even of music and astronomy. Now these same sciences God employed when He made the world. With arithmetic He adjusted it into unity, with geometry He gave it a balanced design upon which depends its stability and its power of controlled movement; with music He allotted its parts that there should be no more earth in the earth than water in the water, than air in the air or than fire in the fire, so that no element could be wholly transmuted into another; whence it comes that the physical system cannot sink into chaos. Some of one element may be transformed into another, but (for example) the air which is mingled with water can never all be changed into water, the surrounding air preventing this; it is this intransmutability that makes possible the mingling of elements. Nevertheless, God has so arranged it that there should be part transmutation of the elements; and when this takes place successively there is brought into existence a new thing that endures in being as long as the agreement of the elements remains. If the agreement is broken the new substance disappears.

God has set up the elements in an admirable order, for He created all things in number, weight and measure. Number appertains to arithmetic, weight to music and measure to geometry. Heaviness is kept in place by the action of lightness—the heavy earth for example is suspended in the middle by the action of fire—and lightness adheres to heaviness as does fire to the earth. In setting up these things eternal wisdom employed an indescribably accurate proportioning. The Measurer of all things foresaw that one element should demand the earlier existence of another and that water should be lighter than earth in the same proportion as air is lighter than water and as fire is lighter than air. Weight and bulk will thus coincide and the container will occupy a larger space than the thing contained. And he related one element with another in such intimacy that one must necessarily dwell in another. The earth, as Plato says, is like some vast animal whose bones are stones, whose veins are rivers and whose hairs are the trees; and the animals that feed among those hairs of the earth are as the vermin to be found in the hair of beasts.

Earth is as to fire as the world is to God, and in relation to the earth fire exhibits many likenesses to God. Its power is unlimited, it appears almighty, penetrating, enlightening, discriminating, and moreover fashioning things with the help of air and water. It is as though of all things that are begotten of earth there was none that did not owe existence to one or other of the activities of fire, and as though the multiplicity of the forms of things reflected the endless variety of the glory of fire. Fire, however, is immersed in things and without them cannot exist; nor can earthly things exist without it. But God alone exists absolutely. Hence was He named of old the absolute consuming fire, God the absolute glory, Who is light and in Whom there is no darkness. His bright and fiery nature all things in their measure strive to share; as we observe in the stars, which exhibit His splendour in material limitation. And this same splendour, dividing and searching through and through, is found immaterially limited in those who live the life of the mind.

Who could help admiring this craftsman who in spheres and stars and in the vast stellar spaces employs such skill that, with no discontinuity, achieves in the widest diversity the highest unity, in one single world so weighing and adjusting the vast bulk and position and movement of the stars, so minutely ordering the distances that lie between them, that each astral area, if it is to be, and the universe, if it is to continue, must be just as it is and in no other way. He gives to each star its own splendour, its own power to influence, its own shape, colour and heat. This heat accompanies its illumination and shares the influence it exerts over other things. And lastly, He in each star so adjusts and proportions the parts to each other that there is in each a movement of parts that secures the whole, downward to the centre in heavy parts, upwards from the centre in the lighter parts, together with a constant movement round the centre; so that we perceive each star to move only through its orbit.

In such a high diversity of endlessly admirable things learned ignorance has taught us never to hope to penetrate to the reasons of all the works of God, but only to admire; for the Lord is great and of His greatness there is no end. He is the absolute maximum and the author and comprehender of all His works, as He is also the end of them all, for in Him are all things and outside Him is nothing. He is the beginning, the middle and the end of all things, the centre and circumference of all that is, and in all things He only is to be sought; for apart from Him all things are nothing. Possessing only Him, we possess all things, for He is all. Knowing Him we know all, for He is the truth of all things. It is His will that the vast admirable contrivance of the universe should lead us to admiration of Him. But the more we accept admiration for ourselves the more are we blinded to the true admiration of Him. For He requires that every heart should in all diligence seek only Him. He dwells in light inaccessible, and it is this light that is universally desired. He it is, therefore, Who can open to them that knock and give to them that seek. Of all creatures that are there is none that has power to disclose himself to the knocker and to show himself as he is—for without Him, who is in all things, creatures are nothing. But to anyone enquiring in learned ignorance what they are, or how, or to what purpose, all things must reply: 'We can answer nothing, we can provide thee with no reply other than nothing, for we know not even what we are; He only knows by Whose intelligence we are that which He wills, commands and knows us to be. Dumb are we all; He it is Who speaketh in all things. He Who made us alone knows what we are, how we are and to what purpose. If thou wouldst know anything concerning us, seek it in our reason and cause, seek it not in us. There, while thou seekest but one, shalt thou find all things. Nor canst thou ever find thyself but in Him.'

'Up, therefore,' says our learned ignorance, 'and find thyself in Him. Then, since all things in Him are Himself, nothing can be wanting to thee. To approach the inaccessible light is not in our power. It is the gift of Him Who gave us the turning of our face towards Him together with the most ardent desire to seek Him. When we have done this, He in His great love will not abandon us but will show Himself to us; and when His glory shall appear, will eternally satisfy us. May He be blessed for ever.'

THE THIRD BOOK

PROLOGUE

WE HAVE SET DOWN THIS MUCH ABOUT the restricted nature of the universe, to the end that we may enquire in learned ignorance into the maximum at once absolute and restricted, Jesus Christ, ever blessed, to the increase of our faith and perfection. Let us further elucidate to your admirable attentiveness, as briefly as possible, the consideration of Jesus. We pray Him Who is truth to be our way to Him, that through faith to fruition we may be made to live in Him, by Him Who is Himself eternal life.

CHAPTER I. THE UNSURPASSABLE MAXIMUM, EVEN IF LIMITED TO THIS OR THAT GENUS OR SPECIES, CAN EXIST ONLY IN THE ABSOLUTE

I N THE FIRST BOOK IT WAS SHOWN THAT THERE endures eternally, equally and immovably itself, an Absolute Maximum incommunicable and never to be contracted or overwhelmed. In the second place was shown the contracted entity we call the universe, for only in limitation can things in plurality hope to exist. The unity of the maximum is absolutely in itself; the unity of the universe is in the restriction called plurality. The plurality of things in which the universe finds its actual limitation could never contain the highest equality; for it would then be no longer in plurality. Things must be distinguished by genus, species and number, or by species and number, or by number simply; that each may repose in its own number, weight and measure. Wherefore are all things separated into degrees, that no two may absolutely coincide.

No limited thing may share in the precise degree of limitation of another; everything necessarily exceeds or falls short of every other thing. All limited things, therefore, have their station between the maximum and the minimum in such a fashion that at any point a larger or smaller degree of limitation may be added. But this process may not be continued to infinity; an infinity of degrees is impossible, for it is no more rational to postulate an actual infinite number of degrees than to postulate no degrees at all; as was shown of numbers in our First Book. In limited things, therefore, it is impossible to rise to the absolute maximum or to sink to the absolute minimum. The divine nature, the Absolute Maximum, cannot be diminished into a finite and limited thing; nor can a limited thing be shorn of all limitation and become the Absolute Maximum.

No limited thing, therefore, since it can suffer further or lesser limitation, can ever reach the confines either of the universe or of a genus or a species. The first general limitation of the total universe is into the plurality of genera, and these branch out into further differentiations. Now genera actually exist only in their species and species only in their individuals; it is these last that alone have concrete existence. As it is admissible to seek the nature of individuals only within the confines of their species, so, conversely, no individual may hope to stretch to the full range of genus and universe; different degrees of perfection must be found among the many individuals of one species. In other words, no individual of a given species can be so completely perfect as to make any higher perfection impossible, nor so utterly imperfect as to exclude the possibility of further imperfection. Nothing stretches to the uttermost confines of its species.

There is but one limit of species and genera and of the universe, and it is the centre, circumference and bond of all things. The universe does not exhaust the infinite and absolutely maximal power of God, like some simple maximum putting a limit to God's power. Consequently the universe does not arrive at the limits of absolute greatness, no more than genera reach the limits of the universe or species the limits of genera or individuals the limits of species. The result is that, between the maximum and the minimum, all things are what they are in the best way possible, with God as the beginning, middle and end of the totality and each member of it, so that all things, whether they rise or sink or tend to the centre, may approach God. That all in their endless variety may be bound together, He makes the bond among them all. Wherefore, among the genera that limit the one universe there is this link between higher and lower that they meet in the middle, and among the different species such is the bond, that the highest species of one genus coincides with the lowest species of the genus immediately above, making one universal and perfect continuity.

The connecting link between species is a thing of degrees and the maximum is never reached, which is God. Therefore species of different genera are not linked by some indivisible third that admits of no greater and less but by a third species whose individuals shade off from one species to the other, no one individual, however, sharing equally both species as being a composite of both. The individual rather shares the nature of its own species in its own individual degree, so that, put side by side with others, it looks like a composite of the higher and the lower species—though never equally of both, for no composite can be formed of exactly equal elements. And placed as it is midway between two species, in its composition one species, the higher or the lower, necessarily prevails. Examples of this are found in the works of philosophers, on oysters, sea shells and other things.

No species then sinks so low as to become the minimum of a particular genus, for before it reaches that minimum it is changed into another; and similarly with species that rise. They, too, change into another before they become the maximal of the genus. When in the genus, animal, the human species strives to reach a high place among beings endowed with sensibility, it is caught up into the new connection of an intellectual nature; but the lower part still prevails, and for that reason it is still named animal. There may well be other spirits—I have mentioned them in *De Coniecturis*—that are broadly classed with the animal because they possess a nature that has something of the sensible in it. But because in them the spiritual nature prevails they are named spirits rather than animals, although the Platonists regard them as intellectual animals. Species, then, must be conceived as being of the nature of an orderly progressive number, necessarily finite, that order, harmony and proportion may characterize the vast variety of creatures, as we pointed out in the First Book. And whether we count down to the lowest species of the lowest genus, than which there is actually no smaller, or to the highest species of the highest genus, than which similarly a greater or higher is not in fact to be found—although still smaller and greater are not possible without postulating a progress into infinity—we must set out from the absolute unity which is God, that our starting-point may be the principle of all things. As we move from the minimum which is the maximum, or from the maximum to which the minimum is not opposed, we shall see species as numbers that meet us on the way. In the universe there is nothing that does not enjoy a certain singularity that it shares with no other. Nothing can prevail over all that is in all things so as to turn their differences into sameness, for never can complete sameness exist in any two things. If at one time one thing is smaller and at another time larger than another, throughout the change it preserves its singularity so that never does it pass through a moment of exact equality. A quadrangle inscribed in a circle may grow to one that encloses a circle, that is, from one smaller to one greater than a circle, without ever touching exactly the same dimension as a circle. An angle of incidence can change from one smaller to one greater than a right angle, without ever touching the mean of equality. More things of this kind will be set forth in the Book of Conjectures.

Individuating principles do not meet in precisely the same harmonious proportion in one thing as in another; every one is meant to be a unity and in its nature perfect. In each species, the human for example, some are counted more perfect and more excellent than others, as Solomon excelled in wisdom, Absalom in beauty, Samson in strength; and those who outclassed their fellows in mental power were deemed worthy of special honour. All this notwithstanding, differences of view following varieties of religion, sects and lands are responsible for different standards of comparison, so that what is praiseworthy here may be odious there. Whence, incapable of an exhaustive study of even one of these candidates for honour, and totally ignorant of the greater number of them throughout the world, it is quite beyond our power to pronounce anyone to be excellent above the rest of mankind.

This is a divine arrangement, in order that each, though he admire others, should be content with the manners of his own people, with his own tongue and all else of his home, and should find something peculiarly dear to him in the soil that gave him birth. In such a spiritual ground there grow unity and peace without envy, as far as may be here below. For this unity is fully present only among them that reign with Him Who is our peace surpassing all understanding.

CHAPTER II. THE MAXIMUM AS LIMITED AND ABSOLUTE TOGETHER, AT ONCE CREATOR AND CREATURE

IT HAS BEEN SUFFICIENTLY SHOWN THAT THE MULTIplicity of the universe is its limitation and that this multiplicity so lies that none of its parts can ever attain to the simple maximum. I will add further that if it were possible for the maximum to become contracted to an actually existing species, this maximum would actually be, according to that contraction, all that it was in the power of that genus or species to become. The absolute maximum is the realization of all possible being and thus is absolutely infinite. The maximum contracted into genus and species is similarly the realization of all possible perfection of that given contraction, and, since a greater perfection of that contraction is not thinkable, it is no less than the infinite embracing every nature of that given contraction. The minimum coincides with the absolute maximum; and the minimum contracted coincides with the maximum contracted.

The clearest illustration of this is to be found in the maximum line. It has no opposite; it contains all figures and is the equal of all the figures it can contain; and, as was shown in the First Book, with it the point coincides. Wherefore, if anything could be presented as the maximum limited individual of a particular species, that thing would necessarily be the plenitude of that genus or species as way, form, reason and truth, in the fullness of perfection of all possibles of that species. Such a contracted maximum, being the final term of every nature within that limitation and including in itself every perfection of that limitation, would, beyond all proportion, hold the highest equality with any given individual, neither greater nor smaller than any, but including in its fullness the perfections of all.

From which it is clear that such a contracted maximum could not exist as a purely contracted thing, for we have already shown that no thing could touch such fullness of perfection in a state of contraction. Nor could such a contraction be God, Who is absolutely illimitable. It would have to be the maximum in a state of limitation, that is, God and creature, the absolute and the limited, and this by a limitation which could only subsist by the subsistence of the absolute maximum. For, as we showed in the First Book, there is only one maximal in which a limited thing could be called the maximum. If maximal power were to unite limitation with itself with the closest union compatible with the preservation of both natures—the limitation being safeguarded which was the fullness of the contracted created species—so that in virtue of the hypostatic union it would be God and all things, such an admirable union would surpass all our understanding. To conceive it as a union of diverse things would be to misunderstand it. The absolute maximum cannot be thought of as other and diverse; for it is all things. To think of it as two things once apart and now united would also be a misconception. For the divine being has no relation to past and future, nor is it rather this thing than that; nor could the limited thing have been describable before the union as this or that, like an individual person subsisting in himself. Neither can the union be described as of parts united to make a whole, for God could never be part of anything. Nor again may anyone conceive this most admirable union as one of form and matter, for the absolute Deity is incapable of being mingled with matter or of informing it.

This union would be higher than all intelligible unions, for here the limited thing—since it is also a maximum—can subsist only in the absolute maximum itself, while it adds nothing to that in which it is, for that is itself the absolute maximum; nor can it pass into the nature of that maximum, for it itself is limited. The limited must here so subsist in the maximum that, if we conceive it as God we deceive ourselves, for the limited cannot change its nature; if we imagine it as creature, we are again mistaken, for the absolute maximum, which is God, does not abandon His nature. If, lastly, we present it to ourselves as a composite of both we are again in error, for between God and creature, between the limited and the absolute maximum, a composition is impossible. We should have to conceive such a being as being at once God and creature, creature and creator—creator and creature both, without composition and with confusion. Who shall be raised so high as to conceive diversity in unity and unity in diversity? Such a union, therefore, would surpass all understanding.

CHAPTER III. HUMAN NATURE AND ONLY HUMAN NATURE PECULIARLY ADAPTED TO BE THIS MAXIMUM

WHAT THE NATURE OF THE CONTRACTED maximum itself ought to be is a question that can be easily solved in the light of our previous remarks. Such a maximum is necessarily one, as the Absolute Maximum is absolute unity; at the same time it is limited to this or that. Now the order of things clearly presents some things as inferior by nature, as lacking life and intelligence, some superior by nature because intelligent, and some between these two. If, therefore, the Absolute Maximum is the most universal being of all things, and not more of one than of another, it is clear that that being is more capable of union with the maximum which shares the nature of the largest number of things.

Consider what would happen if a thing of inferior nature were elevated to the maximum. It would be both God and itself. Let us take the example of a maximal line. That line is infinite in absolute infinity and maximal by the maximum to which it is necessarily united; it is God by its maximality and a line by limitation. It would thus be all that a line could become. But a line does not involve either life or intelligence: which means that a line would have reached the maximum itself, while it lacked the natures above it! It would be the maximum while lacking certain perfections; it could become greater!

A similar pronouncement must be made about the highest

nature that comprises no inferior; for the union of inferior with superior is greater than is either separately. Now, it befits the maximum—with which the minimum coincides—so to unite with one thing that it does not exclude another but rather embraces all. Therefore, a nature in the middle which is the link between inferior and superior is alone most suitable for elevation by the power of the maximal and infinite God. It comprises in itself all natures, the highest of the inferior and the lowest of the superior; so that if it rise together with all that is in it to union with the maximum, it is plain that in it all natures and the whole universe have touched, in every way possible to them, the highest itself.

Now, human nature it is that is raised above all the works of God and made a little lower than the angels. It contains in itself the intellectual and the sensible natures, and therefore, embracing within itself all things, has very reasonably been dubbed by the ancients the microcosm or world in miniature. Hence is it a nature that, raised to union with the maximum, would exhibit itself as the fullest perfection of the universe and of every individual in it, so that in this humanity itself all things would achieve their highest grade. But humanity has no real existence except in the limited existence of the individual. Wherefore it would not be possible for more than one real man to rise to union with the maximum; and this man assuredly would so be man as to be God, would so be God as to be man, the perfection of all things and in all things holding the primacy. In him the smallest things of nature, the greatest and all between, would so coincide in a nature united with the absolute maximum, as to form in him the perfection of all things; and all things, in their limitation, would repose in him as in their perfection. This man's measure would also be that of the angel and of every one of the angels, as St. John says in the Apocalypse (XXI, 17), for he would be the universal contracted entity of each creature through his union with the absolute, which is the absolute entity of all things. From him all things would receive the beginning and end of their limitation. By him who is the maximum in limitation, all things are to come forth into their limited being from the Absolute Maximum, and by means of him revert to the maximum. For he is the first beginning of their setting forth and the last end of their return.

Source or cause of the being of all things, God is the creator of all, and all are made for him. To this highest, maximal and absolute power of creating all things, the nature of humanity would be united. In consequence, God Himself would by this assumed humanity become all things in their limitation in that humanity, as He is the absolute power behind the beings of all things. This man, therefore, since He would subsist by union in the highest equality itself of all being would be the son of God and would be the Word in which all things were made, i.e. the equality itself of all being; and, as was shown earlier, this is what the son of God is called. But He would not cease to be the son of man nor cease to be man, as shall be shown below.

It is in no way incompatible with God, most excellent and most perfect, that these things can be done by Him without any variation, diminution, or any lessening of His nature. It rather fits in with his immense goodness that all things should be created by Him and for Him in the most excellent and most absolutely perfect fashion and in an order suited to its unimprovable perfection. Now this is not so, and no one can reasonably deny, unless he deny God Himself or perfection itself, that all things could be more perfect. From Him who is the highest good and whose work can contain no defect we must put far away every invidious criticism. As He is the maximum, His work, as far as this is inherently possible in creatures, approaches the maximum. But the power of the maximum is exhausted only by and in itself, there is nothing outside it and it is infinite. In no creature therefore could it be so exhausted that this infinite power could not, given any creature whatsoever, create a better and more perfect. But if a man be elevated to unity with this power in such fashion as to be a creature subsisting not in himself but in union with this infinite power, this power terminates not in the creature but in itself. Herein lies the most perfect activity of the maximal power of God, infinite and inexhaustible, and which can never fail; for if it could, there would be neither creator nor creature. For how could the creature exist, as something limited from the divine being, if that very limitation was incapable of union with him? By this creature all things, coming from him who is absolute, are to exist. They in their limitation are from him to whom their limitation is united in the closest union. First, then, stands God the creator. Next is God and man, whose created humanity has been assumed into the most intimate possible union with God, and, as being the universal limitation of all things, is hypostatically and personally united with the absolute power behind the being of all things; that he may exist by the most absolute God through the universal limitation, which is humanity. In the third place all things are in their limited being, so that what they are that they might be in a still better order and manner.

Now this order must not be regarded as a temporal one, as though God had preceded in time the first-born of creation, or as though that first-born, God and man, had preceded the world in time. It is rather an order that by nature and perfection transcends time, so that he who exists with God above time and before all things, in the fullness of time and after many cycles of ages, appeared in the world.

CHAPTER IV. THIS BEING IS JESUS, EVER BLESSED, GOD AND MAN

WE HAVE REACHED THE POINT WHERE, WITH full trust in the deductions we have made, we may hold without hesitation that the conclusions we have set forth are strictly true. We shall now add that Jesus, ever blessed, with the coming of the fullness of time, is the first-born of all creation.

In His earthly life He worked wonders above earthly powers and, found always true in all He said, He affirmed certain things concerning Himself; moreover those who consorted with Him bore like witness and sealed it with their blood. We are, therefore, justified in affirming with unshakable constancy, what indeed has long been proved by irrefutable arguments, that He it is whose coming all creation awaited from the beginning, and who had Himself by his prophets predicted His appearance in the world. He came to fulfil all things. He restored all to health by His will as one having power over all things, He unfolded the hidden and secret things of wisdom, He took away sin like a God, raised the dead to life, transformed nature, commanded spirits, the sea and the winds, walked upon the water and gave to men a law that was the complete fulfilment of all laws. In Him—as witnessed that most distinguished preacher of truth, Paul, enlightened from above in an ecstasy,—we possess every perfection, 'redemption and remission of sins; who is the image of the invisible God, the first-born of every creature, for in Him were all things made in heaven and on earth, visible and invisible, whether thrones or dominations or principalities or powers, all things were created by Him and in Him. And He is before all and by Him all things consist. And He is the head of the body, the Church,

He is the beginning, the first-born from the dead, that in all things He may hold the primacy; it hath pleased Him that all fullness should dwell in Him, and by Him to reconcile all things to Himself.'

Such indeed and many other testimonies of the saints are offered us to the effect that He is God and man. In Him the humanity itself is united to the Word in the divinity itself, so that the humanity does not subsist in itself but in the divinity. Henceforth humanity cannot dwell in perfect fullness except in the divine person of the Son.

In order that we may, above all our intellectual comprehension and as it were in learned ignorance, come to know this person who has united man with himself, let us raise our mind higher and consider the following:

God is in and through all things and all things are wholly in God, as we have already shown. Now these two aspects, both that God is in all and that all are in God, must be taken together and coupled with the fact that the divine nature is of the highest equality and simplicity. Whence, while He is in all things, God is not there by degrees or by a particular measure of communication; and at the same time, because these things cannot be except in diversity of degrees, they are with their natural diversity of degrees in God. In all things and all in Him, God is there, without any variation of His absolute power to create, in unity with the maximal humanity of Jesus; in Him the maximal man cannot exist except in the maximal fashion. Jesus is thus the absolute creative power of God and in Him as in the Son, the middle person, the eternal Father and the Holy Spirit dwell. All things are in the Word; in that most high and most perfect human nature which mightily embraces all creatable beings, all things exist, that all fullness may dwell in Him.

The mind can be gently conducted to the understanding of these things by the following illustration:

Sense knowledge is a limited kind of knowledge; the senses

know only the individual. By comparison with sense-know-ledge intellectual knowledge, which is of the universal, is absolute and abstracted from the limitations of the particular. Now, sensation is found in various degrees of keenness in different animals, and by this they are classed in different grades of nobility and perfection. We have shown that the human, the highest species of the genus animal, cannot rise to the degree which is simply the highest; nevertheless, here the senses behave in such fashion that this animal is also a being of intellect. For man is his intelligence. In him the sense limitation is in some sense supposited in the intellectual nature. While the latter is a kind of abstracted and separate divine thing, the senses remain temporal and corruptible according to their nature.

This bears a certain (though not very close) analogy with what we are now considering in Jesus. In Him the human nature is supposited in the divine, for not otherwise could it exist in its maximal fullness. The intelligence of Jesus, altogether the most perfect in existence, can be personally sup-posited only in the divine intellect, which alone is actually all things. Intellect in man is potentially all things and grows by steps from potency to act, so that the further it grows the less is it in potency. But the maximal intellect, the actually full term of the potency of every intellectual nature, could not exist unless it were also God, who is all in all things. It is as though a polygon inscribed in a circle were human nature and the circle were the divine nature. If the polygon were to become the maximum, than which no greater could exist, it could never exist by itself in finite angles, but only as a circular figure. In consequence it would not have a figure of its own proper being separable even intellectually from the eternal circular figure itself.

The maximal perfection of human nature must be sought in substantial and essential things, in intellect, which the bodily functions serve. Hence the maximally perfect man need not be found eminent in accidentals, but only in intellect. It is not required that he should be a giant or a dwarf or a man of this or that stature, complexion, figure or other accidental. This only is necessary, that his body so avoid extremes as to be a most apt instrument of his intellectual nature, and that it obey without resistance, murmur or fatigue. Our Jesus, in whom even in His earthly life all the treasures of wisdom and of knowledge were hidden as a light in darkness, is credited with having, for the purposes of that most eminent intellectual nature, a body most apt and most perfect, and to this the holy companions of His earthly life bear witness.

CHAPTER V. THAT CHRIST WAS CONCEIVED OF THE HOLY GHOST AND WAS BORN OF THE VIRGIN MARY

IT MUST FURTHER BE CONSIDERED HOW THIS MOST perfect human nature, which now subsists by the subsistence of the Word, does not in any way exceed the bounds of its species, since it is a finite nature at the peak point of perfection. Like begets like, and so the begotten proceeds from its begetter in a similarity of nature. But to a term that is termless there can be neither limit nor comparison. For that reason the maximal man cannot be born in the natural way, and yet the species, of which he is the end and perfection, must have some beginning. His generation, therefore, partly followed human nature, since he is a man. Since, however, he has no causal relation but only a relation of the highest origin to a principle to which he is immediately united, that principle, creating or generating, is his Father, the immediate source of his origin; and the human principle is there as the passive one providing the receptive matter. Hence is he from a mother without male seed.

Every operation proceeds from some kind of spirit and love, uniting the active with the passive, as we have shown somewhere above. Hence the maximal operation, outstripping all proportion of nature, by which the creator is united with the creature must necessarily arise from the highest uniting love, that is, from the Holy Spirit, who is love itself. By him alone, with no help from a limited agent, could the mother conceive, within the latitude of the species, the Son of God. Thus the Father, who fashioned all things out of nothing by the Holy Spirit, so that they proceeded into being from non-existence through Him, now through the same most Holy Spirit achieves this purpose, working a most perfect work.

An illustration may help our ignorance. When some most excellent teacher wishes to reveal his thought in order to feed his pupils with the truth of his mind, he takes care to clothe that thought in sound; thought is not communicable except in a sense-garb. The natural spirit of the teacher fashions the air into an audible shape suited to the thought; the spoken word lives in the thought, so that when it falls upon the ears it reproduces the thought.

The analogy is a slight one, but it does help to raise us in meditation above our natural understanding. The eternal Father, wishing to reveal to us His Son, the Eternal Word, the riches of His glory and immense goodness and the fullness of knowledge and of wisdom, took pity on our weakness. He perceived that only in a sense-form and in one like to ourselves could we grasp the truth, and to make a revelation adapted to our capacity, He clothed His Son in human nature by means of the Holy Spirit, who is consubstantial with himself. And this Holy Spirit, as a word is formed from the air by the breath of man, fashioned the animal body from the pure and fruitful virginal blood, adding reason, that he might be a man, and united the Word of God the Father with this man interiorly, so that the Word became the very centre of subsistence of that human nature. And this was done not in stages, as happens in our human conceptions in time, but instantaneously and timelessly and in accordance with a will at one with infinite power.

No one can doubt that this mother, filled with such virtue and privileged to supply such material, surpassed all other virgins in every spiritual perfection and was endowed with an ampler blessing than all other fruitful mothers. In every way prepared for this single and most excellent virginal childbirth, she was necessarily free from everything that might stand in the way of the purity, the vigour and the unity of so excellent a bringing-forth. For, unless of the most choice and elect virginity, she could not have been capable of virginal conception without the seed of man. If not herself most holy and most highly blessed by God, she could never have provided the workroom of the Holy Spirit in which he fashioned a body for the Son of God. Had she not remained a virgin after this birth, she could not have furnished to this birth a centre of maternal fecundity in its full perfection, but only one shared and diminished and unworthy of the supreme uniqueness of such a Son. Since, then, this most holy Virgin surrendered herself wholly to God and brought to the action of the Holy Spirit the complete concurrence of her most bountiful fruitfulness, there remained with her her virginity, immaculate before birth, during birth and after birth and unsullied above all common natural begetting.

From a Father eternal, therefore, and a mother temporal, the most glorious Virgin Mary, was born Jesus Christ, God and man; from a Father who is the maximum and absolute fullness of being and from a mother of the fullest virginal fecundity and filled in the fullness of time with the highest blessing. He could not be a man, born of a mother, a virgin, except in time; nor could he be begotten of the Father except eternally. But his temporal birth demanded within time the fullest perfection, as it demanded in his mother the fullest fruitfulness.

When, therefore, the fullness of time was come, since a man could be born only in time, he was born in time and in a place admirably suitable, but completely hidden from all creatures. For the divine decrees stand outside all proportion to normal human experiences. Hence was there no indication by which any reason could apprehend these decrees, although in a certain most secret prophetical inspiration divers dark intimations wrapped up in human analogies had been given out, by which wise men might forecast by a process of deduction the incarnation of the Word in the fullness of time. But only the eternal Father foresaw the exact time, place and manner; and he brought it about that, in the depth of the night, when the profoundest silence held all things, the Son should come down from the high citadel into the womb of the virgin and at the most fitting appointed time should manifest Himself to the world in the form of a servant.

CHAPTER VI. THE MYSTERY OF JESUS' DEATH

IT WILL NOT BE OUT OF PLACE TO INTERPOSE HERE A short digression to clarify what has gone before and to enable us the more aptly to set forth the mystery of the Cross. It is beyond question that man is made up of sense and intellect, with a reasoning power between that joins these two together. Order subjects sense to reason and reason to intellect. Intellect is itself not of time and space, but entirely free from them, while sense is completely dependent upon time and space informations. The reason lies as though horizontal to the intellect but at an angle to the senses, that those things that are within and those that are outside time may there coincide.

The senses being animal are quite incapable of understanding things spiritual and outside time. The animal understands not the things of God, for God is a spirit and more than a spirit. Wherefore sense-knowledge is in the darkness of ignorance of eternal things and occupies itself with the flesh and with the desires of the flesh in the concupiscible powers, and with repelling obstacles in the irascible powers. The reason, more noble in its nature because it shares the intellectual nature, is endowed with certain rules wherewith it restrains the passions and desires and reduces them to comparative quietude, lest, placing his whole desire in sense things, a man should be bereft of the spiritual aspirations of the intelligence. It is the first of all laws that a man should never do to others what he would not wish to be done to himself; that eternal things should have precedence over temporal things, and pure and holy things over impure and fleeting things: and the laws framed by most holy legislators from reason itself and promulgated according to divers times and places as counterweights to those who sin against reason, all co-operate to this end.

At a higher level the intelligence recognizes that, even when the senses are subjected to reason by the denial of the passions which are so natural to it, man would still be incapable of attaining by himself the end of his intellectual and eternal aspirations. For man is begotten of the seed of Adam by carnal pleasure which in the act of propagation triumphs over the spirit. And therefore, his nature, originally rooted in carnal delights—for through these did man take origin from his parents—remains quite impotent to transcend temporal things in order to embrace spiritual. Wherefore if the weight of carnal delights drags down reason and intelligence to consent by non-resistance to these movements, it is clear that a man is thereby turned away from God and robbed of the enjoyment of the highest good, which is upward, eternal and of the spirit. If, then, reason controls the senses, it is still more imperative that intellect should control reason, and that in faith fashioned above reason a man should adhere to the Mediator and be drawn by God the Father to glory. No man was ever yet able of himself to rise above himself and above his own nature, so subject from its origin to carnal desire, and, thus freed, ascend to eternal and heavenly things, save He who came down from heaven, Jesus Christ. He it was who also ascended by His own power, for in Him human nature, born not of the will of the flesh but of God, presented no obstacle to His most powerful flight to God His Father.

In Christ then, human nature itself by its union with God is raised to the highest power and escapes the weight of temporal and downward-dragging desires. Christ Our Lord willed to mortify and, in mortifying, to purge out in His own body all those crimes that drag us down to earth, not for His own sake, for He did no sin, but for us; that all men, of the same human nature with Himself, might find in Him complete purification from their sins. That willing and most innocent, that most shameful and most cruel death of the man Christ on the cross was the extinction, satisfaction and purgation of all the carnal desires of human nature. All that is possible to human nature in the way of love of one's neighbour stands out as most generously achieved in the perfect charity of Christ, who gave himself to death even for His enemies.

The humanity of Christ Jesus then atoned for the deficiencies of all men. This humanity, being maximal humanity, embraces the total power of the species and is so much the source of being of each man as to stand far closer to him than ever could brother or most intimate friend. For the maximal of human nature so works that in each man that adheres to Him by formed faith Christ *is* that man in perfect union, while the man's individuality remains untouched. Whence the truth of His own words: 'Whatsoever you did to the least of my brethren, you did to me.' And conversely, whatever Christ

merited in His Passion they also merited who are one with Him
—this in the degree of merit that attaches to diverse degrees of
union with Him by faith formed in charity. Hence in Him are
the faithful circumcised, in Him baptized, in Him do they die,
in Him are they quickened to life again by resurrection, in Him
at last are they united to God in glory. Our justification then is
not from ourselves but from Christ. He is all fullness and therefore if we possess Him we possess all things. It is by formed
faith that we belong to Him in this life; and it is by faith that
we can be justified, as shall be said at greater length later. This
is the ineffable mystery of the Cross and of our redemption, in
which, beyond what has already been touched upon, Christ
shows us that truth and justice and the divine virtues must be
preferred to temporal life, as the eternal before the passing and
perishing. In the most perfect man the highest constancy, cour-
age, charity and humility should dwell, since the death of Christ
reveals the presence of all these virtues in the maximal degree
in the maximal Jesus. The higher, then, a man rises in these
immortal virtues, the closer a resemblance bears he to Christ.
Here the maximal and minimal coincide: maximal humilia-
tion with exaltation, the most shameful death of the virtuous
man with the most glorious life; and so with the rest, all of
which are laid bare to us in the life, passion and crucifixion of
Christ.

CHAPTER VII. THE MYSTERY OF THE RESURRECTION

MORTAL AND CAPABLE OF SUFFERING, CHRIST
could reach the glory of the Father, who, being
absolute life, is immortality itself, only if His mortal
part put on immortality. And this could be done only by
death. How else could mortal put on immortality except by

being shorn of his mortality? and how could that be cancelled except by the payment of the debt of death? Truth itself pronounced those dull and slow of heart who did not understand that Christ must die and so enter into His glory.

We have shown earlier that Christ died a most cruel death for us. It now remains to say that, since it was fitting that human nature should be led to the triumph of immortality by no way but by a victory over death, He underwent this death in order that with Him human nature might rise to eternal life and that animal and body might be rendered spiritual and incorruptible. As true man He must needs be mortal, nor could He convey mortal nature into immortality but in crushing mortality by death.

How neatly Truth itself inculcates this necessity when He says: 'Unless the grain of wheat falling upon the earth die, it remains itself alone; but if it die, it beareth much fruit.' If Christ had remained always mortal, even if He had never died, how could He have bestowed immortality upon the human race? Dying not, He would have continued mortal without death. It was needed, therefore, that he should be liberated from the possibility of death by dying, if He were to bear abundant fruit, so that lifted up He might draw all things to himself; for His power was not only over a world and earth corruptible but also a heaven incorruptible.

Our ignorance may achieve some understanding of this if we keep in mind what was said above. For we showed there that the maximal man Jesus could not have a personal subsistence in Himself separately from the divinity because He is maximal. For this reason an interchange of attributes is allowed in (our speech about) Christ and the human things in Him coincide with the divine. For his humanity is inseparable from his divinity, being indeed in the most intimate union with it; it is, so to speak, clothed in, and caught up into, the divinity and is incapable of separate personal existence. A man consists of body and soul in closest union and the destruction of this union is death. Wherefore the maximal of humanity, whose existence is a divine person's, could not be separated, either body or soul, from that divine person, during the divorce of body and soul called death, for without the divine person the man Christ had no existence.

Christ therefore did not die in such fashion that His person was dissolved. In death there was no local separation from the centre in which His humanity was rooted, and He remained hypostatically united to the divinity. The lower nature, which could suffer the division of soul and body, in the temporal and local sense suffered that division, so that at the hour of death, body and soul were in time and place apart. But corruption was impossible either to body or to soul, for both were united to the eternal. That which was born in time was subject to temporal death and separation, but when the temporal composite had completed the circle of its return to dissolution and the body was now freed from time modifications, His true humanity, which is timeless, remained united incorruptibly with the divinity and reunited as essential His true body and soul. The shadowy image of the true man, which had appeared in time, departed that the true man freed from all capacity to suffer might rise. The same Jesus, now exempt from temporal change and destined to die no more, now most truly rose by the reunion of soul with body, and now lives out of reach of temporal change. True incorruptible humanity could not have been hypostatically united to the divine person without confusion of natures, except by this union of body and soul.

Let Christ's illustration of the grain of wheat come to the rescue of our ignorance and small wit. The grain corrupts numerically while the specific essence remains whole for it is by means of this latter that nature will raise up many grains. If the grain were the maximal and most perfect possible, dying in a most excellent and fruitful soil, it would bring forth not a hundredfold nor a thousandfold but the total possibility comprised in the whole nature of that species. This is what Truth says when He says that it would bring forth much fruit; muchness or multitude is finite, but without number. Consider it more narrowly still. The humanity of Jesus must, in the very thought that it is contracted in the man Christ, be thought of at the same moment as united to the divinity. As united to the divinity it is absolute; as being that concrete man, Christ, it is limited, that through His humanity He may be a man. And thus the humanity of Jesus is as though midway between the purely absolute and the purely limited. Consequently it is only under certain aspects that we can call it corruptible; in itself and apart from particular circumstances it was incorruptible. It was corruptible in the time medium to which it had been contracted; but free from time and above time and united with the divinity, it was incorruptible.

Truth contracted to time is as a sign and image of supra-temporal truth. The truth of the body contracted to time is as the shadow of the truth of the supra-temporal body; and the truth of the contracted soul is as the shadow of the soul freed from time. While it is in time, the soul appears more like sense and reason than intellect; here below it cannot apprehend without pictures. But when it is freed from time the intellect is relieved of the need of pictures. Since Jesus' humanity was supernal, rooted indivisibly in the divine incorruption, at the end of corruptible time the resolution of soul and body could be made only in the direction of that root of incorruptibility. Wherefore at the end of the time-movement—which end is death—when all those things were removed which appertain to the truth of human nature only in its temporal aspect, the same Jesus rose, not with a body of weight and corruption and of the shadowy, passible qualities that belong to composition in time, but with a true, glorious, impassible, agile and immortal body, as was demanded by truth shorn of time-conditions. The truth of the hypostatic union of the human nature with the divine imperiously required this union. Whence Jesus, ever blessed, must rise from the dead as He Himself said: 'It behoveth Christ so to suffer and the third day rise from the dead.'

CHAPTER VIII. CHRIST THE FIRST-FRUITS FROM THE DEAD ASCENDED INTO HEAVEN

FROM THE ABOVE IT WILL READILY BE SEEN THAT Christ is the first-born from the dead. None might rise from the dead before him, since human nature in time never yet attained the maximal or never united as in Christ with incorruptibility and immortality. All men were powerless until he should come who would say: 'I have power to lay down my life and to take it up again.' In Christ therefore, human nature put on immortality; and he is the first-born of them that sleep.

There is but one indivisible humanity and specific essence of all men by which all individual men are men numerically distinct each one from each. The same humanity is that of Christ and of all men, the numerical distinction of individuals remaining unblurred. Hence it is clear that the humanity of all men, who in the temporal order came before or after Christ, has in Christ put on immortality. We may, therefore, patently conclude:—Christ has risen: therefore all men shall rise, when all flow of corruptible time shall cease, and shall be for ever incorruptible. But while there is but one humanity of all men, there are various and divers individuating principles which contract that humanity to this or that subject; and in Jesus Christ alone these were most perfect and most powerful and closest to that essential humanity which was united to the divinity. In virtue of His humanity Christ was able of His own power to rise from the dead; and this power came to His humanity from the divinity, which is why God is said to have raised Him from the dead. Being God and man he rose by His own power, and save Him, no man may rise like Christ, except in the power of Christ, who is also God.

Christ it is, then, by whose human nature our human nature has put on immortality and by whom above time we shall rise in His likeness . . . This shall be at the end of the world, when motion, in which we are born and immersed, shall have ceased. Christ whose birth from His mother only was temporal, did not await the complete flowing away of time before he rose; for time had no comprehension of his nativity. Observe that nature has put on immortality in Christ; wherefore we shall all rise, good and bad, but not all shall be changed by the glory that will transform us into adopted sons by Christ. All indeed shall rise by Christ but not all like Him, and in Him by union; these last shall be only those who are Christ's by faith, hope and charity.

If I mistake not, you now perceive that there is no perfect religion leading men to the last and most desirable end of peace, which does not embrace Christ as the mediator and saviour, God and man, the way, the life and the truth. See what senseless credulity the Saracens are guilty of, who confess Christ to be the greatest and most perfect of men, born of a virgin and caught up into heaven, but deny Him to be God. Blind indeed are they, for they assert the impossible. From what has gone above it must be clearer than light to every intelligent man, that no man could be in all things most perfect and the maximal of man born above nature of a virgin, unless he were also God. But these are senseless persecutors of the Cross of Christ and ignorant of his mysteries. They shall not taste the divine fruit of the redemption, indeed by their law they look not for it; for their law promises nothing but the indulgence of sensual desire. We hope for the crushing out of such desire in the death of Christ; we sigh for the possession of incorruptible glory.

The Jews also like these confess the Messias to be the maximal and most perfect and immortal man but, fixed in the same diabolical blindness, they deny him to be God. They also hope not for the supreme beatitude of the enjoyment of God, as do the servants of Christ; nor shall they achieve it. But, what to me is still more strange, both Jews and Saracens believe that there will be a general resurrection, but do not perceive that it is made possible only by a man who is also God. It might, indeed, be urged that when the movement of generation and corruption ended there could be no perfection of the universe without a resurrection. Human nature is the one essential element in the universe, without which it would be neither perfect nor even a universe, and hence, if time stopped, it would be necessary for men to rise to incorruption, if the whole universe is not to perish. In men, it might be urged, the nature of all mediants is completed, and it would not be necessary that other animals should rise, since man is their perfection. And it might further be submitted that resurrection is necessary that the whole man may receive from a just God the due reward of his deeds. But in addition to all this it is above all necessary to believe in Christ, God and man, by whom alone human nature can attain to incorruptibility.

Blind then are all who believe in a resurrection, and believe not in Christ who alone can make it possible. Faith in the resurrection is in fact the affirmation of the divinity and humanity of Christ and of the death and resurrection of Him who is the first-born from the dead, as was said above. He rose that by an ascension into heaven He might enter into glory. I am forced to conclude that this ascension must be one over all movement of corruption and all influence of the heavens. As God He is everywhere but He is more closely to be associated with that place where never is any change, suffering, sadness etc., such as are found among the things of time. And this place of eternal joy and peace we must assert to be above the heavens, although it is neither conceivable nor describable nor even definable as a place.

He is the centre and circumference of intellectual nature, and since the intellect embraces all, he is above all. But in holy rational souls and in intelligent spirits, who are the heavens that declare His glory, He reposes as in His temple. Thus we conceive Christ to have gone up above all place and all time to His incorruptible mansion, above all that can ever be said, inasmuch as He ascended above all the heavens that He might fulfil all things. As God, He is all in all things; and He reigns in the heavens of those intelligences, for He is truth itself; but not as located, that is, as in the circumference, but as in the centre he sits, for He, as being their life, is the centre of all rational spirits. Wherefore He himself affirms this kingdom of heaven to be also in men, for He is to souls the fountain of life and their last end.

CHAPTER IX. CHRIST, THE JUDGE OF THE LIVING AND THE DEAD

WHO MORE JUST A JUDGE THAN HE WHO IS justice itself? Christ, the fountain-head of every rational creature is Himself the maximal reason, from which flows all reason. Now it is reason's role to exercise discriminating judgment. Hence rightly is he the judge of the living and the dead who with all rational creatures assumed reasoning human nature, and all the while remained God, who is the rewarder of all. Above all time He judges all things by Himself and in Himself, for He embraces all things, being the maximal man, and in Him are all things since He is God. As God He is infinite light in which there is no darkness, and this light illumines all things so that in the light all things are most manifest to the light. And this infinite intellectual light embraces in its timelessness the present like the past and the living as the dead—as bodily light is the hypostasis of all colours. Christ is as the most pure fire which is inseparable from the light, subsisting not in itself but in the light. He is that spiritual fire of life and understanding which consumes all things and involves all in Himself and so, proves, tries and judges all things, like the judgment of the material fire which probes all things through and through. In Him are judged all rational spirits, like all material that is capable of burning. Some such is transformed totally into the very image of fire; like the best and most perfect gold which, remaining gold, is so intensely fired that it seems no longer gold but fire. Other kinds of material like alloyed silver or brass or iron share not such intensity of heat, though all seem transformed into fire, each in its own degree. Now this discrimination is made by the fire only and not by the different materials. For everything soaked in flame apprehends only that most intense heat and not the particular degree of heat it can stand. When we inspect molten gold or silver or copper in very intense fire, their transformation into the form of white heat makes it impossible for us to distinguish these metals. But if the fire itself had a mind, it would understand the degree of perfection of each metal and would adjust its intensity to the nature of each.

Certain ignitable materials can remain indestructible in fire and so, in various degrees of intensity can become capable of shedding light and heat in consequence of their transformation into the very likeness of fire. Others by reason of their alloys can be heated but not to the white heat of light. Christ our Judge, in one most simple and undivided judgment, in one moment most justly and without invidious distinction, communicates to each one, as in the order of nature, not in the order of time, the heat of created reason, that he may pour in upon that reason the light of God's intelligence, so that God be all in all things, and all things in God through this mediator himself, and all grow as much to his stature as their capacities allow. But some, because they are simpler and more unified, can receive both heat and light, others heat in some degree but no light; and all this is dependent upon the capacity of the recipient.

Since that infinite light is eternity and truth itself, it is imperative that the rational creature who desires to be enlightened by Him should rise above earthly and corruptible things and turn to things true and eternal. Corporal things and spiritual things work differently. The vegetative power of a body transmutes the nourishment it receives from outside into the nature of the creature nourished; the animal is not turned into bread, but bread into the animal. But the intelligent spirit, whose action is supra-temporal and, so to speak, upon an eternal level, when he turns to eternal things, cannot change them into himself. Nor can he, as being himself incorruptible, change into them and cease to be an intelligent substance. But he can be transformed into them in such fashion as to be absorbed into a likeness of eternal things; this, however, only in degrees. The greater and more fervent his preoccupation with them the more fully and deeply is he perfected by eternal things, and the more profoundly is his being hidden in the eternal being. Now Christ is more than immortal. He liveth, and He is the life and the truth. Whosoever turns to Him turns to life and to truth, and the more ardently He does this the higher is He raised above mundane and corruptible things to eternal things, until His life becomes hidden in Christ. Virtue is eternal. Justice endureth for ever and ever; and so also is it with truth. He that turneth to virtue, walketh in the ways of Christ, which are the ways of purity and immortality. Virtues are divine illuminations. He, therefore, that in this life turneth by faith to Christ who is virtue, shall be freed from this temporal life and shall be found in the purity of spirit, that he may enter into the joy of eternal possession.

When with all the powers of his mind a man turns by faith to the most pure eternal truth, leaving all else behind, and chooses this truth to be loved alone and loves it, then indeed is there a conversion of his spirit. This conversion by most sure faith to the truth which is Christ means to foresake the world and victoriously to trample it underfoot. To love Him with a most ardent love is to journey towards Him in spiritual movement; not only is He lovable, He is charity itself. When by the steps of love a spirit moves on towards charity itself, it penetrates into charity, not by any temporal movement, but in a manner quite above time and all temporal movement.

Every lover dwells in love: and all that love the truth dwell in Christ. As every lover loves by love, so all that love the truth love it in Christ. Hence none knows the truth unless the spirit of Christ be in him. As it is impossible for a lover to be without love, so it is impossible for anyone to possess God without the spirit of Christ, for in His spirit only are we capable of adoring God. Wherefore unbelievers unconverted to Christ, incapable of the light of glory that transforms, are already judged and condemned to darkness and the shadow of death; they are turned away from life which is Christ. For by His fullness only are all filled with the glory of union. Of this when we shall speak of the Church, founded also upon Him, I shall submit for our consolation some considerations.

CHAPTER X. THE JUDGE'S SENTENCE

IT IS CLEAR THAT NO MORTAL CAN UNDERSTAND THAT judgment and the sentence of that Judge. It is one outside all time and movement; it is not conducted by the weighing of pros and cons, by parallel cases, by discourses and deliberation that involve drawn out session and delay. In the Word were all things made—for, he spoke and they were made—in the Word, which is itself reason, are all things judged. Nor shall there be any interval between the judgment and the carrying it out. Resurrection, final decision, the glory of the accepted sons of God, the damnation and exclusion of souls averted from him, all shall be accomplished in an instant.

An intelligence is above time and unsubjected to temporal corruption, for by its nature it embraces within itself incorruptible forms. Such, for example, are the abstractions of mathematics—and even of physical things, which the mind buries in itself and readily transforms into abstractions or spiritual realities. All this is to us an indication of the mind's own incorruptibility, for the habitat and natural container of incorruptible things must itself be incorruptible. Now this intellect has a natural movement towards the most abstract truth as being the end of all its desires and its final and most delectable object. Now this ultimate object is in all things, for it is God; and the immortal and incorruptible human intelligence is insatiable till it attains him, for it is satisfied only with an eternal object.

But if, freed from the body in which it was subject to the conjectures of time, the intellect reaches not its desired end but falls into ignorance; if, made for truth and in its deepest desire seeking truth not in shadows and signs but rather with certitude and face to face, it now, turned in the hour of its dissolution from truth to the corruptible, pursues corruptible desires, it is rightly said to fall into intellectual death. For it is now occupied with uncertainty and confusion in the dark chaos of mere possibility, in which there is no firm actuality. It is the function of the intellect to know being, and this knowledge is its life. Wherefore, as to know at last the stable, eternal desired object is its life, so is it eternal death for it to be separated from that immutable desired thing and to be thrown into the very gulf itself of confusion where it will for ever, in some way possible to it, be tormented by fire. Its manner of suffering is not to us intelligible other than as the deprivation of its vital nourishment of truth and well-being, together with the loss of all hope of ever attaining to them, so that, without extinction and without end, it ever dies in agony.

This is a life bitter above all imagining, for it is death in life, it is being in nothingness, and knowledge more empty than ignorance. It was shown above that the resurrection of mankind is a rising above movement, time and quantity and all else that is subject to time. Here the corruptible becomes incorruptible, the animal is rendered spiritual, the whole man becomes his intelligence which is spirit and his body (still truly a body) is absorbed into the spirit. The body is no longer in itself as in its corporal and quantitive measurements, but buried in the spirit—a process which is the exact contrary of our state here, where no intellect is seen but only the body, wherein the intelligence seems to be imprisoned. But there the body is in the spirit as the spirit is in the body here; and as here the soul is weighed down by the body, there the body is lightened by the spirit. Hence, just as the spiritual joys of intellectual life are there keenest and in them the glorified body shares, so the sadness of that hell of spiritual death is most terrible, and in it the body in the soul has its share. Our God when apprehended is Himself eternal life and intelligible above all intellect. And therefore, those eternal joys, exceeding all understanding, are greater than words can ever convey.

Similarly, the sufferings of the damned are beyond all thinkable or describable sufferings. All those suggestions of joy, happiness and glory that the Fathers offer us from the analogy of earthly melody and harmony as pointers from things we know to the unknown joys of eternal life, are but pale sense-suggestions, infinitely distant from the truth, of that spiritual good that no imagination can picture. And similarly, the sufferings of hell which they liken to sulphurous fire and pitch and other sense-pains are very faintly described by these analogies, for these sufferings are fiery spiritual agonies; from all which may Our Lord Jesus Christ, our life and salvation, Who is for ever blessed, deign to preserve us. Amen.

CHAPTER XI. THE MYSTERIES OF FAITH

OUR ANCIENT WRITERS ARE AT ONE IN ASSERTING that faith lies at the root of all understanding. In every science certain things must be accepted as first principles if the subject matter is to be understood; and these first postulates rest only upon faith. He who wishes to rise to knowledge must first believe those things without which knowledge is impossible. Says Isaias: 'Unless you believe you shall not understand.' Faith, therefore, embraces every intelligible thing. Understanding is the unfolding of what was wrapped up in faith. The intelligence is therefore directed by faith; and faith is extended by understanding. Without sound faith then there is no true understanding. There is no mistaking the kinds of conclusions that are reached from faulty principles and from a weak foundation: and on the other hand, there is no faith more perfect than that which is founded upon the truth itself, which is Jesus.

Everyone knows that a right faith is the most excellent gift of God. The Apostle John tells us that faith in the Incarnation of the Word of God leads us into truth, that we may become the sons of God. He first sets forth this faith simply and only then narrates many works of Christ in accordance with this faith, that the intelligence may be enlightened in faith. And at the end he suggests the conclusion: 'These things are written that you may believe that Jesus is the Son of God.'

Now this most wholesome faith in Christ, constantly

strengthened in simplicity, can, in our accepted doctrine of ignorance, be extended and unfolded. The greatest and profoundest mysteries of God, though hidden from the wise, may be revealed to little ones and humble folk living in the world by their faith in Jesus: for in Jesus are hidden all the treasures of wisdom and of knowledge, so that without Him no man can do anything. For He is the Word, and the power by whom God made the world, He the most high having alone power over everything in heaven and on earth. He cannot be apprehended within the context of this world. Here we are led by reason, opinion, or doctrine from the better known to the less known by symbols; whereas he is grasped only when movement ceases and faith takes its place. By this faith we are caught up into simplicity above all reason and intelligence to the third heaven of most pure simple intellectuality; that in the body we may contemplate him incorporeally, because in spirit, and on the earth in an entirely unearthly fashion and rather in a heavenly and incomprehensible manner, whereby we perceive that He cannot be comprehended because of the immensity of His excellence. And this is none other than that very learned ignorance—by which the blessed Paul himself, raised higher and into a closer knowledge, perceived that the Christ with whom he was at one time acquainted, he never really knew.

We, then, believers in Christ, are led in learned ignorance to the mountain that is Christ, which our animal nature is forbidden to touch; and when we endeavour to gaze upon Him with the eye of the mind we fall into darkness, knowing that in that very darkness is the mount in which He is pleased to dwell for the sake of all those who live a life of the spirit. But if, in the constancy of a firmer faith we approach Him, we are snatched away from the eyes of them that live by sensuality, to perceive with interior hearing the voices and the thunder and the dread signs of His majesty. We are given to realize that he alone is the Lord whom all things obey. And step by step we come close even to certain incorruptible footprints of Him (as to most divine characters) in which, hearing the voice not of mortal creatures but of God Himself in His holy organs and in the words of His prophets and saints, we come, as in a cloud of more transparent quality, to perceive Him more clearly.

At this point the believer, moving ever upwards in more ardent desire, is caught up into intellectual simplicity and leaps above all sensible things, as though passing from sleep to watchfulness and from hearing to sight; *there* are things seen which cannot be revealed, because they are above all that mortal ever heard and above all the speech of man. For if these revelations came to be told, unutterable things would be framed in human speech, things beyond all hearing would fall upon human ears; for what is there seen is beyond mortal sight. For there is heard incomprehensibly and as surpassing all speech, Jesus for ever blessed, the term of all understanding because He is the Truth, of all sense for He is Life, the finality of all being as He is Being itself, and the perfection of creation for He is God and man. From Him all speech came and to Him it all must return, for all that is true in speech is from Him. For all speech is for instruction, and therefore to Him it must belong Who is wisdom itself. 'Whatever is written is written for our instruction.' Writing is but speech that has been given permanent shape. 'By the word of the Lord the heavens were firmly set up.' All created characters therefore are representative of the Word of God. Spoken word stands for the word of the mind; and this incorruptible word is reason; which is Christ himself, the incarnate Reason of all reasoning; for the Word was made flesh. Jesus therefore is the end of all things.

To the man who rises to Christ by faith such things become clear by degrees. Now the divine efficacy of this faith cannot be explained; for if it be strong, it unites the believer with Jesus so that he ascends above all that is not in union with Jesus. For such a man, if he have full faith in the power of Jesus to whom he is united, exerts a power over movement and nature and commands even the evil spirits; and, as the acts of the saints often witness, marvellous things are wrought, not by him himself but by Jesus in him and through him.

This perfect faith of Christ should be most pure, most intense and, as completely as possible, formed in charity. It does not admit of any admixture or alloy, for it is a faith in the most pure truth that can do all things. Very often in the course of this work we have found the minimum to coincide with the maximum. It is thus with a faith which is simply and purely maximal in act and possibility; it cannot be found in an earthly being unless he be also a heavenly one, as Jesus was. If an earthly soul wished to possess the maximal faith of Christ in pure actuality, such faith would have to be of such indubitable certitude that it were no longer faith but the highest unhesitating certitude in every point.

Here is the all-powerful faith which is the maximum and the minimum and embraces all that is to be believed in him who is the Truth itself. And if the faith of one man does not attain the degree of another's because equality is impossible—just as a thing seen is not seen as exactly the same by several different people—this nevertheless is essential, that each one believe to the full power of belief that is in him. Then, even if he exhibit by comparison with others the faith only of a grain of mustard seed, so great is the power of that faith that it exacts obedience from the mountains themselves; for it commands by the power of the Word of God, to whom he is, in his measure, strongly united by faith: and none can resist that power.

Such by the power of Christ will become the force of your intellectual spirit, if it adhere to Him above all things and be so nourished by Him and be so one with Him by union as to become—its individuality always reserved—as it were, supposited in His life. But if this is brought about only by the complete turning of the spirit—which draws the sense with it—to

Him in strongest faith, that faith itself must be formed in unitive Charity. Complete faith is not possible without charity. Every living thing loves life and every intellect loves to know. How then could Jesus, immortal life itself and infinite truth, be believed in and not loved with the most ardent love. Life of itself is lovable; if Jesus therefore is believed to be eternal life, it must be impossible not to love Him. For faith without charity is not living faith but dead, and ultimately, not faith at all. But charity is the form of faith and that which gives it true being; indeed it is the sign of the most unshakeable faith. When all things are abandoned for His sake, when body and soul themselves are reckoned as nothing by comparison with Him, then have you certificate of a most powerful faith.

Nor can faith be strong without the holy hope of enjoying Jesus. There would be little surety in a faith that did not hope for the promises of Christ. If a man does not hope to possess the eternal life which Christ has promised to believers, can he be said to believe in Christ? Can he be said to hold Christ to be the truth? If he has not an unshakable hope in the promises, how could he choose death for Christ, having no hope of immortality? It is because he holds that Christ abandons none that hope in Him, but bestows upon them eternal beatitude, that the believer judges it well to suffer all things for Christ and to await so great a reward for so little.

Great indeed is the power of faith which fashions a man in Christ's mould so that he foresakes sensible things, denudes himself of the contagions of the flesh, walks in fear in the way of the Lord, follows in the footsteps of Christ with joy, and willingly and even exultantly takes up the cross. Such a one is as a spirit in the flesh; to him for Christ's sake this world is death, and life lies in its removal that he may be with Christ. Of what spirit is he in whom Christ dwells by faith? What is that amazing gift of God which by faith raises us, poor pilgrims in frail flesh though we be, to such power above all that is not Christ by union. Let us brace ourselves that each one aspire by daily mortification to rise by steps to union with Christ, even, as far as may be, to the deep union of absorption in him. Such a one, leaping above all visible and mundane things, reaches the complete perfection of his nature.

Here is the perfected nature which, the flesh and sin being destroyed, we may attain in a transformation into the image of Christ. This is far removed from those occult practices of certain necromancers who claim that a man may be raised by faith to a close union with a spirit who is his familiar, and by the spirit's power be able to work wonders in fire or in water, to effect strange transformations with the help of magical musical incantations, or to reveal the closest secrets of nature. It is quickly recognized that in all these things the soul is seduced and turned aside from life and truth. Such souls become completely fettered to these dark spirits and their faith issuing in deeds they offer them, with incense, the worship that belongs only to God. This worship they discharge with abject reverence and much incantation, as to one capable of granting their requests. And their trust does sometimes bring them their earthly desires; but they are held close to a spirit to whom, divided eternally from Christ, they will for ever adhere in torments.

God be praised that he has by his Son redeemed us from the darkness of such ignorance and has taught us that all is false and a lie, howsoever produced, that comes to us from any other mediator than Christ who is the truth, and from any other faith but that of Jesus. There is but one Lord Jesus, the master of all things, who fills us with every blessing and who alone makes ample satisfaction for all our deficiencies.

CHAPTER XII. THE CHURCH

THE NATURE OF THE CHURCH MAY BE GATHERED from what has gone before but I shall add a brief word upon it to complete this work.

Faith of necessity enters into and dwells in different souls in different degrees; and no man may hope to attain the maximal faith, than which no greater could exist, as similarly none can reach the maximal charity. Maximal faith, than which none could be greater, if it dwelt in a soul here below, would at once render him a sharer of the beatific vision; for the maximal in any genus, as it is the ultimate terminal of that genus, is thereby the initial point of the genus next above. Whence maximal faith can simply not be in any man who is not also in the state of comprehensor. Similarly maximal charity cannot be in a lover who is not at the same time the Beloved Himself. Whence neither faith nor charity in the maximal degree are predicable of any man but of Jesus Christ, Who is both viator and comprehensor, at once the man who loves and the God who is beloved. Within the maximal are all things included for it embraces all. In the faith of Jesus Christ, all true faith and in His charity all true charity are comprehended, each in its distinct degree. These distinct degrees lying below the maximum and above the minimum, no man, even if he possess, as far as could be, the maximal faith of Christ, could reach that maximal faith by which he might comprehend Christ, God and man. Nor could any man so love Christ that he could not possibly be loved more; for Christ is love and charity itself and consequently infinitely loveable. No one, that is, could either here or hereafter love Christ so much as to become Christ and man. All then who are united to Christ either by faith and love here below or by taste and embrace hereafter, are united to

166

Him in a particular degree, and this degree determines the intimacy of the union; and none subsists in himself apart from this union, nor does the union destroy the individual's degree.

Now this union is the church, the gathering together of many into one, as the many members are gathered into one body, each in his own degree. One member is not another, but each with the others is one body which unifies them all. None can enjoy life and existence apart from the body, while none can claim to be the body except as dwelling in the body. While we journey here below the truth of our faith can subsist or continue to be only in the spirit of Christ, while the order of believers remains a high diversity in agreement, in one and the same Christ. And when we sink out of the church militant at death, we shall afterwards rise only by the power of Christ, so that the church triumphant shall also be one, with each in his own hierarchical niche. Then shall the truth of our flesh be not in itself but in the truth of the flesh of Christ, the truth of our body shall be in the truth of Christ's body, and the truth of our spirit in the truth of the spirit of Christ Jesus, like the branches of the vine; so that there shall be but one humanity in all, the humanity of Christ, and one spirit, that of Christ, in all spirits, and that each may dwell in him in such fashion that there is but one Christ in all. Hence, in this life to receive one of all that are Christ's is to receive Christ, and to do unto the least of His is to do unto Him. To wound Plato's hand is to wound Plato; if a foot is caught in the smallest snare, the whole man is thereby caught. In the heavenly country to rejoice in anything however small is to rejoice in Jesus and to see Jesus in everything: for by him is God ever blessed. Thus by His Son shall our God be all in all things, and each member in His Son and through him united with God, and with all things, that joy may be full without envy or any defect.

While we sojourn here our faith can continually increase as can also charity. Each it is true is in such a degree that at a given moment and given his nature he may not be in another; but while he is in one degree he is in potency to another, though never in potency to the infinite charity of Christ. But we must, by the grace of our Lord Jesus Christ work to actualize our total possibility, and to move from virtue to virtue and from degree to degree, by him who is faith and charity. Of ourselves, as ourselves, we can without him do nothing. But all that we can do, we can do in him who alone can make up for our deficiencies, that in the day of resurrection we may be found to be integral and noble members of him. Believing and loving with all our power, we can confidently beg of Him this grace of increased faith and charity, in tireless prayer approaching His throne with great trust. For He is infinitely merciful and loving and permits none to be defrauded of His holy desire.

Dwell upon these things as they are, and you shall be flooded to the depths of your soul with a gracious sweetness of spirit and shall scent the inexpressible goodness of God in an interior taste and most aromatic incense, which, passing, He will minister to you; and with which you shall be satisfied when His glory shall appear. You shall be satisfied, I repeat, and with no disgust of satiety, for this immortal food is life itself. And as the desire to live increases ever, so the food of life is eaten ever, but never to become the nature of the partaker. That food sets up disgust which oppresses the stomach but does not bestow immortal life, for it fails of its nature and becomes the nature of the feeder. But the desire of our mind is to live by mind, which is continually to enter more and more into life and joy. But life and joy are infinite; and the blessed are borne into life and joy by ardent desire. They who drink of the fountain of life are satisfied in such fashion as still to thirst; and as this drink never becomes a past thing, for it is eternal, ever are they blessed both drinking and in thirst, and never shall that thirst and its satisfaction pass.

Praised be God who has given us a mind that cannot be

satisfied with the temporal. Its desire having no limits, it recognizes itself as above all time immortal, from its insatiable desire within time. It perceives that it cannot be satiated with the desired intellectual life except in the fruition of the most excellent and highest good that can never fail. The enjoyment of that good can never become a thing of the past, for appetite can never grow less. To offer an illustration from the body, it is as if a starving man sat at a great king's table, to be plied with the one food that he longed for, the nature of which food was to sharpen the appetite the more it filled. If such food never gave out, it is clear that in being filled, the feeder would continue to long for the same food and be ardently moved to continue to seek it. A man would always long for a food whose power was to stimulate the feeder to seek it with greater and greater desire. Such is the power of an intellectual nature, that receiving life into itself, it is transformed into that life, to the degree of its power of transformation. The air which receives into itself the ray of the sun becomes itself light. The intellect becomes the thing it understands; but it understands only the universal and incorruptible and enduring things, for incorruptible truth is its object; and to this is it by its nature moved. And this truth it apprehends in the still peace of eternity in Christ Jesus.

Such is the Church Victorious in which is our God for ever blessed. There is Christ Jesus, true man, united with the Son of God in such supreme union that the humanity has no foothold in existence except in the divinity: and in such ineffable hypostatic union that the truth of his humanity could not bear a deeper or more simple union and continue to be. Furthermore, if every rational nature were in this life turned to Christ in deepest faith and hope and charity, while the personal reality of each remained intact, all would be so united to Christ that all, angels and men, would have no existence apart from Him. By Him the reality of the body of each one is to be drawn in and absorbed in God through its own proper spirit, so that each one of the blessed, the reality of his own being untouched, should be in Christ, Jesus Christ Himself, and through Him God in God, and that God Himself, remaining the absolute maximum, should be in Christ Jesus, Jesus Himself, and the all in all things through Him.

In no other way can the Church be completely one. For the church means the unity of the many, with the preservation of the personal reality of each, without confusion of natures or degrees. Now the more the church is one, the greater she is. But this Church is the Church at its greatest possible point. This Church then the Church of the eternally triumphant is the most vast because a greater union in her is not conceivable. Gaze deep into this union where the union is absolutely maximal and divine, and where is found the unity of Godhead and humanity in Jesus and the unity of the Church of the victorious blessed with the Godhead of Jesus. Nor is absolute unity itself greater than the unity of the natures in Jesus or of the blessed in heaven. For it is the maximal unity, which is the union of all unions and that which is all unions, receiving neither less nor more, and proceeding, as was shown in the First Book, from unity and equality. Nor is the union of the natures in Christ greater or less than the unity of the church triumphant, since, being the maximal union of natures, it suffers in this neither greater nor less.

Whence all diversities that become united take their unity from that very maximal union of the natures in Christ. By this, the unity of the Church is what it is. But the unity of the Church is the maximal ecclesiastical unity. And being maximal, it coincides with the hypostatic union of the natures of Christ above it. And the union of the natures in Jesus coincides with the absolute unity which is God. Thus the unity of the Church, which is the union of subjects with her, although it does not seem as perfect as the hypostatic union, which is one of natures only, or as the first divine simplicity, in which no otherness or diversity could exist, is nevertheless resolved by Jesus into the divine unity from which it first took its rise. This shall be better seen if we recall what has often been insisted upon earlier. The absolute unity is the Holy Spirit. The maximal hypostatic union coincides with the absolute unity. From this it follows that the union of natures in Christ is by the absolute, which is the Holy Spirit, and exists only in it. Now, as we have shown, the unity of the Church coincides with the hypostatic union; whence, in the spirit of Jesus, who is in the Holy Spirit, lies the union of the triumphant souls in heaven. So says Truth itself in St. John: 'The glory which thou gavest me I have given to them; that they may be one as we are one, I in them and thou in me, that they may be made perfect in one.' In consequence the church in eternal peace will be so perfect that it could not be more so, and so transformed in the light of glory that in all things only God shall appear. To this church of so great love and triumph do we aspire, imploring God the Father Himself with suppliant hearts that by His Son, Our Lord Jesus Christ, and in Him by the Holy Spirit, that He would grant us of His immense love this union, that we may eternally enjoy Him Who is for ever blessed.—Amen.

LETTER OF THE AUTHOR TO THE LORD CARDINAL JULIAN

TAKE NOW, REVERED FATHER, WHAT FOR LONG I have by divers paths of learning sought to attain. Attainment, however, was denied me until I was returning by sea from Greece, when, by what I believe was a supreme gift of the Father of Lights from Whom is every perfect gift, I was led in the learning that is ignorance to grasp the incomprehensible; and this I was able to achieve not by way of comprehension but by transcending those perennial truths that can be reached by reason. In union with Him who is the Truth, I have now set forth the learning that is ignorance in these books, and these can be reduced or enlarged from the same source.

In these most profound matters every endeavour of our human intelligence should be bent to the achieving of that simplicity where contradictories are reconciled; and this is the scope of the First Book. From that point the Second Book follows a path higher than that commonly pursued by the philosophers and makes a few deductions on the universe which many will find unusual. And now, at last, I have finished the Third Book on the ever-blessed Jesus. In this I have worked always from the same principle and, by an increase of faith, I have steadily grown in knowledge and love of the Lord Jesus. No one who believes in Christ can deny that in this way his longing for Christ becomes more intense, so that after long prayer and meditation he sees the most sweet Jesus as the one fitting object of his love and joyfully leaves all else to embrace Him who is true life and everlasting joy. All things are credible to one who thus approaches Jesus. No scriptures can cause him difficulty, neither can this world, since this is transformed into Jesus on account of the spirit of Christ which dwells in it; and He is the end of the intellect's desires. Do you, therefore, devoted Father, pray to Him earnestly and continuously for me that we may together enjoy Him in eternity.

Completed at Cusa, in the year 1440, the 12th day of February.

www.ingramcontent.com/pod-product-compliance
Lightning Source LLC
Chambersburg PA
CBHW030827090426
42737CB00009B/912